"In a single publication, Chantal Sicile-Kira has sensitively combined personal interviews and the extensive literature highlighting personal perspectives into a thoughtful collection of comments that address topics ranging from sensory integration to employment. I would highly recommend this book for anyone who lives with, works with, or educates someone on the autism spectrum."

—Dr. Cathy Pratt,
chair of the board of directors for Autism Society of America
and director of Indiana Resource Center for Autism

"Chantal Sicile-Kira does an excellent job explaining important life skills topics in a clear and concise manner. The book provides insight into many of the challenges faced by teenagers and adults on the autism spectrum."

—Stephen M. Edelson, PhD,
director of Autism Research Institute

"No parent-author of a significantly affected child with autism has listened, and learned, from adults on the spectrum more than Chantal Sicile-Kira. In this perhaps her most useful book, she shows us how these long-ignored experts have greatly enhanced her ability to help her son Jeremy achieve a happy and purpose-filled life. Brava, Chantal."   —Michael John Carley,
executive director of GRASP,
The Global and Regional Asperger Syndrome Partnership, Inc.,
and author of *Asperger's from the Inside Out*

"Wonderfully practical and totally diverse, *Autism Life Skills* generously gives voice to a wide range of people right across the autism spectrum who demonstrate that whatever the nature of one's autism in an ocean of autisms, many basic and essential life skills can be attained by tuning in to individual differences and shaping empowering and inclusive pathways accordingly."

—Donna Williams, DipEd, BA Hons,
bestselling author, artist, and autism consultant

continued . . .

"*Autism Life Skills* is a collection of truths you will turn to again and again. Chantal is a teacher of talent, and as a father of two boys with autism, I feel fortunate to be in a privileged position to be a better parent by reading her book and absorbing her wisdom."　　—Edmund C. Arranga, founder of Autism One

"Essential reading for any caregiver or educator who wants to see children with autism reach their full potential. The poignant and deeply personal accounts from individuals living with autism yield invaluable, practical life skills that will offer hope to countless families."

—Suzanne Wright, cofounder of Autism Speaks

"The many moving personal stories from adults on the spectrum in Chantal's books provide much-needed insight into the children we are raising and educating today. Both parents and educators will gain more understanding of what it is like to have autism, and learn how we can best prepare our children for adulthood. I highly recommend this excellent book."　　—Lee Grossman, president and CEO of Autism Society of America

"In her best work yet, Chantal went straight to the source—people on the autism spectrum—to answer some of the most vexing questions related to helping those with autism lead fulfilling and productive lives to the greatest extent possible. Thank you, Chantal, for providing a venue for the voices of people with autism to be heard regarding what skills and qualities are needed for success!"

—Stephen M. Shore, EdD, author and autism consultant,
Board of Autism Society of America,
and Board of the Asperger Association of New England

"Sicile-Kira orchestrates a meaningful balance between fundamental information, personal experience, professional perspectives, and the many voices of individuals with autism. A useful and insightful book!"

—Valerie Paradiz, PhD, author of *Elijah's Cup*

"Chantal Sicile-Kira's book is an excellent resource for anyone wondering how best to help both children and adults on the autism spectrum. In these pages, you will find a treasure of insights for preparing autistic children for life."

—Zosia Zaks, MS, MEd, CRC,
disability advocate and author
of *Life and Love: Positive Strategies for Autistic Adults*

Autism
Life Skills

From Communication and Safety to
Self-Esteem and More—10 Essential Abilities
Every Child Needs and Deserves to Learn

CHANTAL SICILE-KIRA

A PERIGEE BOOK

A PERIGEE BOOK
Published by the Penguin Group
Penguin Group (USA) Inc.
375 Hudson Street, New York, New York 10014, USA
Penguin Group (Canada), 90 Eglinton Avenue East, Suite 700, Toronto, Ontario M4P 2Y3,
Canada (a division of Pearson Penguin Canada Inc.) • Penguin Books Ltd., 80 Strand, London
WC2R 0RL, England • Penguin Group Ireland, 25 St. Stephen's Green, Dublin 2, Ireland
(a division of Penguin Books Ltd.) • Penguin Group (Australia), 250 Camberwell Road,
Camberwell, Victoria 3124, Australia (a division of Pearson Australia Group Pty. Ltd.) •
Penguin Books India Pvt. Ltd., 11 Community Centre, Panchsheel Park, New Delhi—110
017, India • Penguin Group (NZ), 67 Apollo Drive, Rosedale, North Shore 0632, New
Zealand (a division of Pearson New Zealand Ltd.) • Penguin Books (South Africa) (Pty.) Ltd.,
24 Sturdee Avenue, Rosebank, Johannesburg 2196, South Africa

Penguin Books Ltd., Registered Offices: 80 Strand, London WC2R 0RL, England

While the author has made every effort to provide accurate telephone numbers and Internet
addresses at the time of publication, neither the publisher nor the author assumes any
responsibility for errors, or for changes that occur after publication. Further, the publisher does
not have any control over and does not assume any responsibility for author or third-party
websites or their content.

First edition: October 2008

Library of Congress Cataloging-in-Publication Data

Sicile-Kira, Chantal.
  Autism life skills : from communication and safety to self-esteem and more—10 essential
abilities every child needs and deserves to learn / Chantal Sicile-Kira. —1st ed.
    p. cm.
  Includes bibliographical references and index.
  ISBN 978-0-399-53461-4
  1. Autistic children—Life skills guides. I. Title.
  RJ506.A9S536 2008
  618.92'85882—dc22   2008021584

PRINTED IN THE UNITED STATES OF AMERICA

10 9 8 7 6 5 4 3 2

PUBLISHER'S NOTE: Neither the publisher nor the author is engaged in rendering
professional advice or services to the individual reader. The ideas, procedures, and suggestions
contained in this book are not intended as a substitute for consulting with your physician. All
matters regarding your health require medical supervision. Neither the author nor the
publisher shall be liable or responsible for any loss or damage allegedly arising from any
information or suggestion in this book.

Most Perigee books are available at special quantity discounts for bulk purchases for sales
promotions, premiums, fund-raising, or educational use. Special books, or book excerpts, can
also be created to fit specific needs. For details, write: Special Markets, Penguin Group (USA)
Inc., 375 Hudson Street, New York, New York 10014.

For Maman and Papa

What is important is not what happens to us,
but how we respond to what happens to us.

—Jean-Paul Sartre

The unrealized potential of my dreams
makes me master of my future.

—Jeremy Sicile-Kira

CONTENTS

ACKNOWLEDGMENTS

Many people were instrumental in writing this book. I am most grateful to all those adults and teens on the spectrum who gave freely of their time and allowed me to pester them with questions either in person, on the phone, or via email. They shared details of their lives so that parents and educators could understand more about how they could help the children of today prepare for the future. Many expressed the hope that others would not suffer through the same situations they had, and that they would have a more positive experience growing up. I am also grateful for the personal stories that parents and educators shared with me during my travels to conferences and seminars around the country. I value the trust that people have placed in me.

Thanks to James Levine, my agent, for his guidance, and Marian Lizzi, my editor, for being exacting with her pen, making this book more readable and more useful.

When I needed a quiet place to write and no responsibilities to distract me, the Ranglas family, owners of the Del Mar Motel and the Poseidon Restaurant, came to my rescue, and for that I am thankful.

For their continual support to Jeremy, I am grateful to the Afternoon Angels: Dana Pulde, Mark Grichanik, and Joe Medrano. Thanks to Jeremy's friends Andrea and Andi for taking the time to get to know him. Thanks to Janine Dupree and Maureen Shull, instructional aides, for establishing a great rapport with Jeremy, teaching him so well, and for always being there for him. Thanks to Matt, Vivian, Kristi, and Jeff, the "newbies," for their patience in learning how to best support Jeremy in reaching his goals.

There is one person who has made the most impact on my son these last four years, Allan Gustafson, Jeremy's high school teacher. Allan is the person most responsible for Jeremy becoming the mature, reflective young man he is today. Allan inspired Jeremy to believe he could attain his dreams of getting his diploma, going to college, and earning a living. Allan taught him also that making those dreams come true requires taking responsibility and working hard. I could never possibly thank Allan enough for all that he has given to my son. Every teenager should have such a mentor.

Others who play an important role in my son's life and have my appreciation include Phylinda Clark-Graham, case manager, and Debra Plotkins, educational consultant, both with San Diego Regional Center; and Dr. Nora Baladerian, psychologist.

Thanks to Bruce Cochrane, director of Pupil Services at San Dieguito Union High School District, and Carl Fielden, learning disabilities specialist at Grossmont College; Dawn Holman, clinical director of Autism Spectrum Consultants; Chris Vinceneux, clinical director of School Options; and Brooke Demner, occupational therapist.

Thanks as well to Dana Berchman and Craig D'Entrone User, producers of the MTV *True Life* episode "I Have Autism." Their portrayal of autism as experienced by three different people on the spectrum (including Jeremy) was respectful and thoughtful, and did wonders for Jeremy's self-esteem during a difficult time in his life.

Many thanks to all my friends and family for their support. Extra thanks go to Veronique, Katrina, Valerie, and Francine for always being there.

Finally, I am forever grateful to my husband, Daniel; my daughter, Rebecca; and my son, Jeremy, for their love, patience, and understanding.

FOREWORD

One thing I really like about this book is that Chantal Sicile-Kira has done a beautiful job of putting the voices of many people on the spectrum into one book. In my own life I have found reading other personal accounts very helpful. When I was a child, loud noises hurt like a dentist's drill hitting a nerve. I was relieved to learn that other people with autism had similar problems with sensory oversensitivity. When I was little I thought other people could withstand the noise because they were stronger than me.

The first part of this book describes the different sensory oversensitivity problems that many individuals on the spectrum have. Sensory problems can be extremely debilitating. They can make it *impossible* for a child or adult to tolerate places such as a large supermarket or noisy classroom. When behavior problems occur, especially in a nonverbal individual, the first question that one should ask is, "Is the problem sensory or behavioral?" Some of the things that are most likely to cause sensory overload are flicker from fluorescent lights, shrill high-pitched sounds such as smoke alarms, and over-stimulatory places such as shopping malls. Perfumes and smells of detergents and other chemicals can also cause problems. There are some individuals who will never tolerate a large supermarket. Some individuals can be desensitized and become less sensitive while others cannot. Sensory oversensitivity problems are highly variable. For example, one child may be attracted to the sound of running water and others may run away screaming.

This book also covers transition to adult life. People often look for a single magic turning point. There is no single turning point; a teenager or adult on the spectrum can keep gradually improving. When I was a teenager the people who helped me the most were my aunt who had a ranch and Mr. Carlock, my high school science teacher. I was a poor student in high school because I saw no point in studying. Mr. Carlock motivated me to study by showing me that graduating from high school and going to college would enable me to fulfill my goal of becoming a scientist. He also gave me formal instruction on how to research scientific journal articles.

I have interviewed many parents whose son or daughter on the spectrum has had great success in the job world. In most cases there was a slow transition from the world of school to the world of work. Kids need to start getting work experiences way before they graduate from high school. They need to learn skills such as being on time and doing things that other people want them to do. They need to start learning job skills *before* they graduate. When I was in high school I started a sign-painting business and worked on my aunt's ranch. In college I did summer internships at a research lab and a school for autistic children. Individuals who make a successful transition into the world of employment are often "apprenticed" into their jobs.

Many successful computer programmers who have Asperger's were given formal instruction in programming when they were in middle school. They needed the formal instruction of being taught by either their parents or a teacher who took an interest in them. Kids will mess around on computers and play video games, but they need to have lessons to get turned on to career-relevant skills with computers. I call this "lighting the fuse." Once the student is turned on by a good teacher, he will often study on his own, but he needs a mentor to get the process started. This principle applies to all types of job skills. The lessons also teach the concept of doing an assignment that will satisfy the needs of *other* people.

Another essential skill that must be taught is how to take turns. This was drilled into me as a child by playing board games such as Chinese checkers and card games such as hearts, old maid, and poker.

At a recent autism meeting, I had an interesting conversation with a parent who came from India. She said that the many kids labeled Asperger's in the United States are the ones who have bad behavior, but they are smart. The emphasis in India is in developing skills so they will be employable. We need to take the person's area of *ability* and develop it. Too often there is too much emphasis on deficits instead of building up the areas of strength.

One of the characteristics of people on the spectrum is that skills are uneven. They will be good at one academic subject and bad at another. Visual thinkers like me who think in photo-realistic pictures often have problems with algebra, but they may be able to do geometry. The pattern thinkers who think in mathematical patterns may often excel in math and music but may have problems with reading. The third type is a word thinker who may memorize hundreds of facts but has problems with visual thinking tasks.

When a child is getting ready to leave middle school and go on to high school, parents and teachers need to start working on what will he do and how will he be cared for when school is over. I have seen too many individuals on the spectrum successfully graduate from high school and college totally fail in the work world. This was due to either a failure to develop this area of strength into employable skills or a lack of basic skills such as grooming and hygiene, being on time, or making rude comments about the appearance of customers. One of the advantages of my 1950s upbringing was that basic manners and skills were pounded into all children.

Parents and teachers often ask me how to handle a child's obsessions and special interests. Use the tremendous motivation of the special interest to motivate learning useful things. If the child likes trains, read a book about trains. An obsession with insects could be turned into a career in entomology. Be creative.

The people who helped me the most were teachers who had some Asperger traits themselves.

—TEMPLE GRANDIN
Author of *Thinking in Pictures*

ABOUT THIS BOOK

Many people have strong opinions about the importance of words and how we label one another. In describing people and situations, I have tried to use words that the individuals prefer. In doing so, I hope that I have not inadvertently offended anyone, and if I have, please forgive me.

I have used "neurotypical" or "nonautistic" or "off the spectrum" to describe people who are not diagnosed with an autism spectrum disorder.

I have used mostly "on the spectrum" and "autistic" and "Aspie" to describe people who are diagnosed with an autism spectrum disorder.

Some names have been changed for those who wanted to share their experience but wished to remain anonymous.

To be practical, I have mostly used the pronoun "he," sometimes "she," and sometimes both. However, in most cases, unless I am speaking about a gender-specific issue, I'm speaking about both male and female individuals.

The term "Afternoon Angels" refers to the wonderful people I have hired and trained over the years, who help teach and support Jeremy, usually in the afternoon and on weekends. Raising a son like Jeremy requires a team approach, and the Afternoon Angels are a very important part of our lives.

INTRODUCTION

TEACHER: What are your greatest dreams about your future?
JEREMY: I want to have my own house with roommates, good friends, and fun job and be learning.

TEACHER: What are your greatest fears about your future?
JEREMY: That I will not have enough money.

TEACHER: What barriers might get in the way of accomplishing your goals?
JEREMY: You know I need good helpers. I need people that respect my intelligence.

> —Allan Gustafson, interview with Jeremy Sicile-Kira,
> spring 2007

It's 5:00 a.m. and I'm up writing at the time of day I love best—everyone is asleep and the phones aren't ringing, and if I don't check my email, I know I can actually get a few solid hours of uninterrupted writing done. Except today, it ain't gonna happen.

I hear someone lumbering down the stairs, and it's my son, Jeremy, followed by Handsome the dog, and the two cats. Jeremy, who at eighteen usually has a hard time getting up at 7:00 to get ready for school, is heading for the refrigerator. He opens the fridge, pulls out a big chunk of cheese, and brings it over to me, grinning from ear to ear. "I want cheese, please." I get a knife, cut a few pieces for Jeremy, and put the cheese away. I ask him to go back upstairs to bed.

Ten minutes later, and he is back down again. I ignore his presence and continue typing. He circles around the dining room table where I am sitting. He hovers, and finally taps me on the shoulder and verbalizes, "I'm hungry." "Okay, what do you want?" I ask, handing him his letter-board. "I think we have some rice left over from dinner and we have bagels." Jeremy spells out, "u r nice to make some rice." "With butter and salt?" "Yes," he says. He gets a plate out, I get the rice and butter out of the fridge, we heat up the food, and he sits down to eat. When he is done, he stands up and hovers over me (I'm back at my computer) and starts stimming. "What is it now, Jeremy? Why are you up so early, why don't you go back to bed?" Jeremy spells out, "I don't like that Mary Jeanette is gone. I like her and I am worried about her baby."

The amazing thing is that none of this would have been possible a few years ago. Over the last four years, Jeremy has learned a new way to communicate. He has learned to recognize his emotions and put them into words. When he is worried about his new teacher who had to go on maternity leave earlier than anticipated because she needed complete bed rest, he can tell me. When he is happy to see a former tutor who is back in town on a visit, he can express that to her. When he is frustrated by the difficulty of a physical activity, he can tell his occupational therapist that he doesn't know how to move his body. Best of all, he is developing friend-ships with people his own age, since he can finally communicate with them.

Although Jeremy still faces major difficulties in functioning inde-pendently in his daily life, he has shown us that he is capable of learning some of the basic life skills we all need. Abilities such as communication, establishing social relationships, good self-esteem, the ability to recog-nize and control his emotions (self-regulation), telling us how he feels and what he wants (self-advocacy) are a few he is learning to use. None of this would have been possible without the seeds that were planted when he was a child, through years of hard work, both at school and at home.

Those who have seen Jeremy on the documentary series *True Life*, in the award-winning episode called "I Have Autism," will remember how challenged Jeremy is by his autism, how difficult it is for him to do just about everything. Nothing has come easily to him. Yet you will also remember his can-do spirit, how he wants to be able to connect with other people, he wants to make friends. And he is determined to do that despite the barriers he faces.

During his last two years of high school, Jeremy spent much time discussing with his teacher, Allan Gustafson, about what he wanted his future to look like. They were planning his transition program. He is very clear about his goals: to live in his own apartment, have his own business, go to college and continue learning, and have friends. We all had to think about what Jeremy would need to learn in order to live the adult life he wanted. This made me reflect upon all the work he had done, all the efforts we had made to get him this far along.

I realized that, if I had the chance to do it over, there are some things I would have done differently—hindsight is always 20/20. When Jeremy was born, there were not the options there are now, and there was not as much knowledge about how to help a child on the spectrum.

As I pondered this, I began to wonder: What would adults on the autism spectrum—those severely impacted by autism as well as those with Asperger's syndrome—point to as the most important influences when they were growing up? What, in terms of what they learned and how they were treated as a child, has made an impact on the adults they are now?

Through my speaking engagements around the world and my consulting, I have been lucky enough to meet and develop relationships with a wide range of individuals on the spectrum. So I decided to ask them what the essential life skills were in their eyes, and how they had learned them. I also asked them to think about what they wished they had known when they were children. I also read almost every book written by a person on the spectrum, and visited many of their websites and blogs to find out what others were thinking. The result is this book.

As the saying goes, *When you've met one autistic person, you've met one autistic person.* I interviewed all kinds of people with different functioning levels—those considered by neurotypical standards "less able" and "more able." I interviewed people who were diagnosed when they were children, and people who were diagnosed as adults, as well as those whose diagnosis followed that of their child's. Yet despite all their differences, common threads emerged and the same skill areas kept coming up in conversations; skills that were important to them now, yet were challenging to them as children. There were different aspects of each skill that were problematic, depending on where they were on the spectrum, but there were more similarities than differences.

The ten skill areas that kept coming up form the ten chapters of this book. Sensory processing (making sense of the world), communication, and safety were the top three areas people wished they'd received help with as children, followed by all the others. Many continue to have some difficulties in certain areas. Most had strong opinions about what they wished they had been taught when they were little. Practically all had definite opinions about what was helpful and what was not while they were growing up.

Why is this important to us as parents and educators? Because as you read these stories, you will recognize a bit of your child or student in some of them, and you will understand more about why he acts or reacts the way he does. These personal stories will offer some ideas for you to try to help your child or student. All the adults I interviewed hoped that the children of today would not suffer as they did because of lack of knowledge. They hoped that children would benefit from their experience. Every child we are raising or educating is a future adult, and now we have the opportunity to benefit from the real experts—adults who have been there—and find out what we can do to best prepare our children for real life.

It was not until I started talking to people that I realized how safety was a daily concern for them, as children and for many still now as adults. Imagine how much safer and more secure we can help each child be, just by learning from others' experiences and applying some lessons learned. I don't think that most of us take into account how impacted all on the spectrum are by sensory processing difficulties, and knowing that will help us change the way we teach and approach each child. It also can help us figure out how to develop a system of communication for the nonverbal child.

All these skills are necessary for all children, yet too often we are so busy teaching children on the spectrum their ABCs and their 123s, as well as sitting, listening, and "look at me" skills, that we forget that they are, first and foremost, children. We need to teach them the basic life skills all children need to learn along the way, that children on the spectrum do not pick up through osmosis. Skill areas such as self-esteem and self-advocacy and earning a living are major areas of concerns to adults on the spectrum. Many parents and educators start thinking about these skills in high school. Of course, it is never too late to learn, as many of the stories in this book demonstrate. But clearly, it would make life much easier if they were given some of the tools as children to start the foundation of what they will need more and more as time goes by.

Our children are all different, and our dreams and hopes for each are not the same. Many parents may be focusing on "recovery" for their child. Even so, these children—whether they end up staying on the spectrum or not—will still need these essential life skills. To what degree and how will look different for each person. Their potential may be different, and the strategies to teach them may differ, but the intent is the same: to build a foundation, providing each child with what he will need to know to live happily, productively, and responsibly as an adult.

Sit back and enjoy reading what the real experts in this book have to say. You'll come away with more insights into your child or student and some ideas about what he needs and deserves to learn. I hope and expect that you will feel empowered by the insights these uniquely knowledgeable experts have shared.

1

Sensory Processing:
Making Sense of the World

Jeremy often states he has difficulty with areas related to movement and it is evident. Environment plays such a big part of Jeremy's life. From lights being too bright, to his sense of smell and places being too noisy, these barrages from his surroundings limit his capabilities to coordinate mind and body. When we think of all the things us adults have to do, Jeremy finds these activities extremely arduous.

TEACHER: *How do you learn most easily?*
JEREMY: *Hearing.*

—Allan Gustafson, interview with Jeremy Sicile-Kira,
spring 2007

When Jeremy was a baby, he had low muscle tone. I did not think he was developing normally, but it was not until he was a year old that I could get any professional in France, where we then lived, to agree. Then we started physical therapy and we taught him everything—how to put his arms out to break a fall, how to get into a sitting position, how to roll over, and eventually how to crawl and how to walk. When he finally took his first steps, they weren't toward me or his father; he just followed the pattern in the rug, over and over again. It was then I knew for sure he had autism.

When we walked around Paris, he would stop at every café and store-front and stare at the Visa and American Express decals in the windows. If left to his own devices, he would stare at the same picture in his favorite French picture dictionary. He also loved to twirl objects and put his face as close to the spinning object as he could get without stopping its orbit. His favorite object was a Chinese spoon that had a design imprinted on it that he would intently stare at while it spun on the table. When we moved to England, we lived in a two-story house. Whenever Jeremy descended the stairs, he would run the bottom of his foot on each step as if he was feeling his way down.

Jeremy loved to listen to me read to him in both French and English. In England, we lived under the flight pattern for the Concorde, and I remember that once he learned the word "airplane," he would say it about thirty seconds to a minute before any of us would hear the plane very far away. It was the same with dogs barking: he could hear a dog bark before we ever did.

Now, with hindsight and with all the information on autism that's available today, I see clearly what Jeremy's behaviors were telling me about how or what his senses were processing (or not), and I can now follow the clues that would have helped me figure out how to help my son. If I had known back then what to look for, I would have realized that my son was an auditory learner and that his visual processing was not working well at all. Back then, professionals were not much more knowledge-able about autism than I was when it came to understanding the connection between autism, sensory processing, and learning. We were told our son was severely autistic, that he was retarded, and that we should find a good institution for him. No one explained that if his sensory processing was out of whack, that could be why he was not learning. Thank goodness we all know more now and we can help young children earlier and more easily.

The Most Important Skill of All

This chapter is the longest one in the book, and the most important for understanding the difficulties children on the spectrum have. Making sense of the world, understanding what their senses are telling them—that is, understanding what is going on around them—is what most adults on the autism spectrum convey as the most important skill they needed to learn as children. In fact, it is the most important skill *all* children need to learn. Unless a child understands what it is he is seeing, hearing, touching, feeling, and smelling, how can he learn any other skill necessary to survive in today's world? Communication, self-esteem, safety, self-regulation, self-care, and earning a living are a few essential skills that first require an awareness of the world, as well as awareness of oneself in that world.

However, helping a child make sense of the world requires that we, in turn, try to understand how she perceives her surroundings, and how we can help her best. It requires patience and perseverance and a willingness to help her processing (sensory and emotional) so she can learn and function, but without judging her on her differences or perceived functioning level. It requires that we accept and believe that a lack of understanding on the part of a child on the spectrum has nothing to do with intelligence, but everything to do with sensory processing and how that affects learning.

Today, there are many options to help people overcome their processing challenges: biomedical and dietary interventions, sensory integration, auditory training, visual processing programs, behavior modification, and more. Not all of these will work for everyone. Finding out what has helped adults on the spectrum to make sense of the world is helpful in giving us ideas for our children today. More examples of how adults learned how to cope will be given in Chapter 6, "Self-Regulation."

How Babies Learn: The Importance of Our Seven Senses

Imagine looking at a face, yet seeing only an eye or a nose or at best a Picasso-esque portrait of a person. Imagine feeling pressure in your midsection but not knowing if it means you need to use the restroom, or you are very hungry and you need to eat, or that you are sick and will soon vomit. Imagine not being able to feel your arm and your leg at the same time, or trying to coordinate your body when you can't feel your body parts. Imagine your hearing is so sensitive that you can't make out what people are saying because of the overwhelming background noise, or that your sense of touch is so sensitive that clothes feel like sandpaper. These are just a few examples of what children on the spectrum may experience, in varying degrees.

Most adults on the autism spectrum report having had sensory challenges as children, and most continue to have these challenges in adulthood. The intensity of the challenge and which senses are affected vary for every individual. Many older adults with Asperger's syndrome were diagnosed only later in life (some only when their own children were diagnosed), and so it is only now that they understand the "why" behind the difficulties they experienced as children or even now as adults.

For most children, the saying "I feel, therefore I am" aptly describes them. Babies first learn to make sense of their world by exploring their environment in different ways. At first they are just touching and grasping with their little hands, then mouthing what is given to them, and then they start to make sense of what they are hearing and seeing. As the months go by, they start exploring the environment around them more and more, reaching for toys, moving their bodies around. For neurotypical babies, this stage of exploration is essential because it is how they learn to make sense of their world. What they come to know about their environment is based on how their brain is processing the information given to them through their senses. How we interpret our environment through our senses affects every aspect of our lives. It is through our senses that we recognize the emotions in others, that we develop a sense of self-awareness, and that we learn to communicate with and understand other people.

Amanda Baggs is autistic and a disability rights activist as well as a blogger who became an Internet sensation after she posted videos on YouTube about how she experiences the world. She has been highlighted on CNN and elsewhere. Having someone like Amanda able and willing to share with us nonautistic parents and teachers about what it is like when you have processing difficulties is truly helpful in trying to understand what some children on the spectrum may be going through and how we can help.

Amanda communicates by typing, uses a wheelchair to get around, and has many sensory processing challenges. Although Amanda's body responds to what is around her, it's not always the specific responses that nonautistic people expect to see. She says that every time she sees an autistic person, she is struck by how much awareness that person seems to be indicating to various things around them, but how oblivious nonautistic people seem to be to that awareness. This is an example of how behavior *is* communication, but we are not always so good at picking up on what the message is. Amanda reports having trouble planning deliberate physical movements, a challenge which is shared by many on the spectrum.

Sensory processing challenges can look different in different children depending on what sense is most affected. A child on the spectrum with distorted sensory processing will have a different interpretation of what he "sees" or "feels" or "hears." For each person, the sensory challenge and therefore the interpretation will be different, as it is for each of the blind men in the Asian parable of the "Six Blind Men and the Elephant." Each blind man feels a different part of the elephant and has a different interpretation of what an elephant is. The blind man who feels a leg says the elephant is like a pillar; the one who feels the tail says the elephant is like a rope; the one who feels the trunk says the elephant is like a tree branch; and so on. Each child is like a different blind man, with different challenges in how his senses perceive the world.

Sensory Processing Disorder

Well-known authors on the autism spectrum such as Donna Williams, Temple Grandin, Liane Holliday Willey, and Stephen Shore have described how sensory processing disorder affected their development as children, their ability to get through the day, and their relationships with others. Other less-well-known authors and bloggers, as well as people I have interviewed, have validated these experiences as being shared by all.

PRACTICAL TIP

Some children who have been doing well in general education classes may start to encounter difficulties in the third or fourth grade. This is the time when teachers start assigning projects that have to be done over a period of time (i.e., not turned in the next day) and when students are given more responsibility. Assignments are no longer predictable or handed to them; they need to check the blackboard as well as listen to the teacher's instructions. Good teamwork between teacher and parents is important in helping the child develop organizational skills and overcome any monochannel challenges he may have. Making sure the student is given assignments in written form, teaching him to color code on a weekly planner the project deadline and when he will work on it, and reminding him to follow his planner every day is a good way to help the student focus and learn skills that will serve him well over his lifetime.

Sensory processing disorder is described as the inability to process information received through the senses. What this means is that the different senses are not working the way they do for nonautistic people. A child may be oversensitive (e.g., the child who arches his back and becomes stiff as a board when you try to hold him) or undersensitive (e.g., a child may have cut himself and be bleeding and not react at all, as if he does not feel the pain). One child's visual processing may be affected, whereas for another it might be his auditory processing, and yet another child may have difficulty with both.

Some children may be "monochannel," meaning they can process through only one sensory channel at a time. This means that a child may be able to process information he is hearing, but not process what he is looking at, and vice versa. For example, in general education classrooms, students are often required to copy down the assignment written on the chalkboard while the teacher begins lecturing on that day's lesson. A child who is monochannel will not be able to process what he is hearing while he is visually processing the assignment he is copying down, and he will miss out on the lesson. An easy fix in such a case is to give the assignment to the student on a piece of paper so he can then pay full attention to what the teacher is saying.

Making Sense of the World According to Adults on the Spectrum

Tito Mukhopadhyay is severely impacted by autism and yet is the author of several books, including *The Mind Tree: A Miraculous Child Breaks the Silence of Autism*. His mother, Soma, developed the Rapid Prompting Method (RPM) in order to help her son reach academic success and communication. Tito's book provides an insightful glimpse into what it is like to have severe autism. For example, Tito describes his struggle to use more than one of his senses simultaneously. Motor planning difficulties are also explained in such experiences as trying to ride a tricycle. Tito says that he tried to order his legs to move (to peddle the bike), but that they would not move. His mother had to do a lot of hand over hand with any tasks requiring muscle groups, such as teaching him to ride the tricycle. I remember her telling me how she sat him on a chair, and over and over for most of the day, she would put her son's legs through the motions until he could move them on his own.

My son, Jeremy, has the same problem as Amanda does in terms of planning deliberate physical movement, and as Tito did in getting his muscles to work. When Jeremy was little, I had to teach him every physical action by motoring him through them. Years later, when trying to teach him something that requires any kind of motor activity, I still need to motor him through it repeatedly, quickly and often, as if his muscles are creating motor memory.

If you have a child with a history of low muscle tone who does not follow through with verbal instructions, do not assume that he does not understand. He may be experiencing motor planning and initiation challenges as described by Amanda, Tito, and Jeremy. Perhaps using some of the techniques that have helped Tito and Jeremy and people like them will help your child.

Body Awareness/Self-Awareness

Most people are familiar with the sensory areas of touch, sight, hearing, smell, and taste. Less well known, but just as important, are the vestibular and the propioceptive senses. The vestibular sense has to do with where our body is in relation to the surface of the earth, while the propioceptive sense has to do with where our limbs are in relation to the rest of our body. You may have noticed that many children on the spectrum are not that interested in sports. Those who are fully included in physical education class may have difficulty with many of the activities. Part of what can be challenging is the social aspect of games like soccer and baseball, but part of it is that many children on the spectrum are clumsy and are not comfortable playing sports, all related to challenges in body awareness involving the propioceptive and vestibular senses.

Brian King, LCSW, is a licensed clinical social worker and autism consultant who was diagnosed with Asperger's syndrome at age thirty-five, soon after his son was diagnosed in fourth grade. In conversation with Brian, as well as through his informative website, www.ImAn Aspie.com, Brian shares what having Asperger's is like for him in terms of body and spatial awareness. He describes how difficult it is for him because the part of his brain that determines where his body is in space (propioception) does not communicate with his vision. This means that when he walks, he looks at the ground because otherwise he would lose his sense of balance. Driving produces similar challenges for Brian, and he watches the road or the back of the car in front of him when he is driving in order to maintain the feeling of being grounded. In either case when he looks up or around him, he loses the sense of where he is.

Donna Williams, bestselling autistic author and self-described "Artie Autie," has published nine books, produced paintings and sculptures, and composed music. Donna had extreme sensory processing challenges as a child and still has some but to a lesser degree. Some of her books are memoirs about her life with autism and some are textbooks with advice on how to teach a person with autism. All of the books are fascinating, giving detailed accounts of what life is like with sensory pro-

---

PRACTICAL TIP

If a child is unable to perform or initiate a motor task when asked, try physically prompting her through the physical gestures repeatedly until her body starts to respond. Then you can begin to gradually decrease the prompting. If a child has toileting accidents, take data not only on variables such as when she ate and drank and how often, but also on the sensory environments in which the accidents occur. If the sensory environments are linked to the toileting accidents, make a behavior plan for desensitizing the child to certain environments over time, as well as providing toilet training.

---

cessing difficulties, and provide real insight into the world of someone who is highly intelligent but has struggled all her life to be able to "feel" her body and to make sense of the world around her, and even herself. In her memoirs, including *Like Colour to the Blind*, Donna describes how she has a hard time feeling what her body is telling her, what it needs, and where the boundaries of her body are in space. Children who are tapping themselves may be trying to "feel" their bodies. Donna talks about feeling a sensation in her stomach area, but not knowing if it meant her stomach hurt because she was hungry, or if her bladder was full. When she looks in a mirror, she sees pieces of herself, not a whole.

Last year, she posted a blog on her site www.donnawilliams.net that she finally could run a bath independently at the age of forty-three (see Chapter 7, "Independence"). Her past experiences of running baths included overflowing bathtubs, burning water she could not feel, and not knowing what order to put her body into the bath. As a teenager, she took showers but used to burn herself and leave the shower running for hours. When living on her own at the age of fifteen, she had major problems with bath taking. She tried all sorts of tactics, such as putting on a timer, but then she would leave the timer in another part of the house and not hear it. Before that she would burn herself because she could not feel when the water was too hot. This body awareness piece is just a bit of what sensory challenges Donna has had to overcome with a variety of therapies and techniques including biomedical intervention and diets (see "Food for Thought," later in this chapter).

Some adults on the spectrum have told me that this body awareness is very important to understanding the world around them and is a necessary part of self-awareness. Self-awareness of who one is, where one's body begins and ends in space as well as what one is feeling, is much needed to have self-esteem and be able to engage in self-advocacy.

Touch Sensitivity

Another area of challenge for some on the spectrum is touch sensitivity. Temple Grandin, arguably the world's most famous autistic woman, author of *Thinking in Pictures*, *Animals in Translation*, and *Developing Talents*, has mentioned in her talks how she hated to wear certain clothes. Scratchy petticoats and new underwear and bras were like sandpaper on raw nerve endings. Temple suggests that parents can avoid many sensory-induced tantrums by dressing kids in soft clothes that cover most of the body. I would also suggest removing clothing tags as those can be irritating as well.

Like Temple, Brian King finds that light touch feels irritating and can cause him to become defensive, especially when he doesn't know it's coming. He prefers deep pressure such as from a firm hug or a deep massage. When someone touches him lightly, he needs to rub deeply to erase the tickle or itch brought on by the light touch. He is anxious about people standing close to him, as he is afraid they will touch him lightly. Like many on the spectrum, Brian reports that showers are hard to handle because the drops feel like pin pricks on his skin.

Stephen Shore, who was diagnosed with atypical development with strong autistic tendencies and was nonverbal until the age of four, is the author of a few books including *Ask and Tell* and *Beyond the Wall*. If you have ever seen pictures of him, you will note that he is always bearded. Shaving feels like using a power sander on his face, so his way of dealing with it is to not shave.

Auditory Processing

Many adults on the spectrum report having had auditory processing difficulties as children. Donna Williams describes having very tumbled receptive information processing and the memory of a goldfish, yet she stored huge strings of sound patterns and sang and chattered to herself most of the time, often in stored lines, jingles, and advertisements. In other words, her condition helped her develop a highly refined capacity to sense pattern shifts; a great natural capacity for mimicry, parody, and characterizations; and a seemingly bottomless memory for stored strings of information.

Similarly, auditory comprehension works differently for Amanda Baggs than it does for most people. It takes a conscious effort to understand what people are saying. Without the conscious effort on Amanda's part, people's voices sound like running water. Amanda says she comprehends more reliably by noticing patterns of sounds, rather than focusing on the meaning of words as most people do.

In 2004, Daniel Tammet became a sensation when he memorized and recited more than 22,000 digits of *pi*, setting a worldwide record. Daniel, author of *Born on a Blue Day: Inside the Extraordinary Mind of an Autistic Savant*, sees numbers, shapes, colors, and textures, and can perform amazingly difficult calculations in his head. He can learn to speak new languages fluently, from scratch, within a week. Yet Daniel remembers that, as a child, learning in class did not come easily. He found it difficult to concentrate when the other children were talking among themselves or people were walking in the corridors outside. Daniel found it hard to filter out external noise and used to regularly put his fingers in his ears to help himself concentrate. One of his brothers has the same problem and uses earplugs whenever he wants to read or think.

Michael John Carley, the executive director of GRASP (Global and Regional Asperger Syndrome Partnership) and author of *Asperger's from the Inside Out: A Supportive and Practical Guide for Anyone with Asperger's Syndrome*, says that he has to lock in and focus on whom or what he is listening to—for example, if his wife talks to him from another room, he may not hear her. His son also shares this trait.

PRACTICAL TIP

When considering your child or student in his environment, or when you are doing a functional behavioral analysis because of challenging behaviors, take into account factors such as the clothes the child is wearing, the light and noise level, and how people are physically handling and touching him.

It is interesting to note that there seems to be extremes in the same person in terms of processing difficulties and extraordinary talents. For example, as a child, Daniel Tammet had trouble focusing on learning because his hearing was so sensitive, yet as an adult he can teach himself a language and be fluent in one week. Donna Williams had very mixed up auditory processing as a child, but as an adult she can compose and play music.

As parents and teachers, we want to help our children learn as much as possible. It is reassuring to know that some individuals who, as children, did not have access to the therapies and strategies we have today were still able to make sense of their world and even develop talents as adults in what were areas of difficulty in childhood. Now, we have techniques such as auditory integration training and the Listening Program, among others, to help us help our children.

Eye Contact

Eye contact can be difficult for different reasons. For some children on the spectrum, it is uncomfortable to look at someone's face because they get mesmerized by seeing various parts of the face moving, which causes them to lose focus on what the conversation is about. Many on the spectrum have learned to look at a point at the bottom of the person's ear or at a spot on the wall behind his head, so they don't get distracted from listening to what is said.

Brian King says that making eye contact does not come naturally to him, and that after long conversations, he is exhausted and anxious from the constant attempt to keep up the eye contact. Since being diagnosed with Asperger's, he understand why this is difficult for him, and now he either does not engage in prolonged eye contact or he wears sunglasses with polarized lenses.

Michael John Carley also experiences some difficulty in making eye contact, but not as much as when he was a child. Because he needed to focus and lock into what he was hearing, he usually aimed his ear toward the person he was listening to, and he wonders if this isn't a part of the lack of eye contact he had as a child.

Visual Processing

While visual processing may be a factor in why some children on the spectrum find eye contact difficult, it has an enormous effect on how we interpret and interact with the world. Visual processing is extremely important for eye-hand coordination, how we move in space, and especially for learning. Most of our teaching techniques are visually based. If a child is unable to make sense of what he is seeing because his visual processing is not working correctly, it will be a serious challenge for him to learn.

Many children are overly sensitive to light. My son and others on the spectrum have explained to me that they cannot "feel" their body when it is too bright. Turning off some of the fluorescent lights or sitting near a window with natural light is helpful to them. Many adults wear baseball caps and/or tinted glasses indoors to offset the effects.

There is a misconception that all children on the spectrum are visual learners. This is simply not true. We have no way of knowing, unless we try to teach differently, if a person we think of as unteachable, or unable to learn, is really someone who is not processing visually, but can learn through his auditory processing.

Tito Mukhopadhyay underwent testing with Dr. Michael Merzenich, a neuroscientist at the University of California at San Francisco Medical School. In one test of perception, when Tito was presented simultaneously with light and sound, he could not see the light, unless it was presented a full three seconds after the sound. Tito has explained that he can process only one form of sensory input at a time (monochannel) and has chosen to use his auditory processing.

■   ■   F O O D   F O R   T H O U G H T   ■   ■

THE IMPORTANCE OF VISUAL PROCESSING TO UNDERSTANDING

The journalist asked about our tinted lenses. I took them off and described the room. The relatedness of things disappeared and everything was now a conceptually and unrelated entity. The "on" and "next to" and "in front of" didn't mean much anymore, because whatever something was "on," "next to," and "in front of" no longer had a reality until it was focused upon directly. The reviewer's face was again in unrelated bits. A toy bear that had been sitting on a table next to a lamp now became cognitively disconnected from its surroundings, which was no longer processed or taken account of . . . The words for things failed me and were defined instead by their size, shape, textures, sounds, materials or by their use or relationship to other things or people around them. . . . the pen became a long thing for writing . . . the interviewer's hand was now conceptually disconnected from his body in all but theory . . .

—Donna Williams, *Like Colour to the Blind* [1]

■   ■   ■   ■   ■   ■   ■   ■   ■   ■

Jeremy, my son, used to, as a child, run his feet over the steps going down the stairs. Now when I ask him why he did that, he says that he couldn't see where the step began and ended, so he needed to feel where the edge of the step was.

Temple Grandin is well known for being a visual thinker and she credits her visual processing for having the talent she does in being able to draw and design livestock-handling facilities. On the other hand, Donna Williams talks about the inability to make sense through her visual processing and that as a child she saw only patterns and colors. In *Like Colour to the Blind*, Donna describes what it was like when she put on tinted glasses (Irlen Lenses), that all of a sudden the colors and patterns in the room actually became the window, the curtains, the furniture, and so on. Those lenses helped her interpret what her processing could not.

When my son was a child, his therapists and teachers used a lot of visual strategies to try to teach him. I remember when we started to use very simple social stories with him, for example, the three expectations of good behavior in the library, he did well when we read the rules to him and he did not look at the written instructions. Eventually the teachers and I realized his auditory processing, although sensitive, worked far better than his visual processing.

Nowadays, there are options to help children with their visual processing. Vision therapy may be an option for some. Wearing tinted glasses may help as well for some children.

Orientation Mobility

Liane Holliday Willey, who was diagnosed as an adult following the diagnosis of her daughter, is the author of *Pretending to Be Normal: Living with Asperger's Syndrome*. Liane has many challenges with sensory processing, and in her book she describes how her visual processing affects her orientation mobility. She finds it very difficult to pick out objects from a background and to judge distance. She cannot rely on her own perception, especially under the duress of sensory overload. This greatly affected her ability to navigate and find her way around when she was a college student. She describes how the crowds of students between classes blocked her ability to see the landmarks and points of references she used to get around campus, and that the noise would overwhelm her. When she began teaching at the college level, she loved her job, but she hated the fact that the campus was in a congested and noisy part of town. Having to drive to get there in itself was a challenge for her: the humid climate assaulted all her senses, and she had to focus on changing gears (she had a manual transmission), making sure she did not go the wrong way down one-way streets.

Brian King remembers the difficulties in switching from elementary school to junior high. One of the major difficulties for him was that he had to change classrooms, which he did not have to do as an elementary school student. Brian found it a real challenge to get used to the school schedule. On his class schedule, which he carried around for a month because he could not remember the order of his classes, he wrote down

■   ■   F O O D   F O R   T H O U G H T   ■   ■

HOW DR. BERNARD RIMLAND AND BIOMEDICAL INTERVENTIONS HELPED ME

Donna Williams, PhD, is a bestselling autistic author who has written a total of nine very helpful books, including *Nobody Nowhere*, *Like Colour to the Blind*, and *Autism: An Inside-Out Approach*. Here is what she has to say on her blog at http://blog.donnawilliams.net about how Dr. Bernard Rimland and biomedical interventions have helped her sensory processing:

Bernard Rimland had time for people. And he made time for me. When Nobody Nowhere, *the first of my 9 books in the field of autism came out, Bernard befriended me over the phone and I finally met with him in person in the US. I would call him Bernard Rimland and he would remind me to call him Bernie, but I never did. He was a warm, jolly, earthy human being who saw me as I wished to be seen, not a famous person, just a person with autism among many people with autism.*

Being one of the first mainstream published cases of a person with autism dealing with immune deficiency and dairy, gluten and salicylate intolerance (and dairy allergy), Bernard wrote a foreword to Nobody Nowhere *at a time when the autism stereotypes were of silent sullen middle class boys and still too narrow and archaic to easily embrace a working class girl with a vast repertoire of songs, advertisements and jingles who had been labelled psychotic in infancy, disturbed throughout childhood and finally diagnosed with autism in early adulthood.*

When I learned new things that might help others dealing with metabolic, gut and immune disorders, I shared it with Bernard. When I went onto an amino acid/anti inflammatory/smart drug called Glutamine and after 30 days experienced my first conscious experience of a simultaneous sense of self and other, I phoned Bernard excitedly, overwhelmed, shocked at this new cognitive experience and what it finally taught me of society. "I have touched the heaven of shared social," I burbled to Bernard down the phone. "I know what it is to be with . . . not 'at,' not 'in front of' but 'with.'" Today, hearing Bernard Rimland has passed away, I'd like to share with the world that this man worked so hard for physically ill children with autism (and not all people on the autistic spectrum are physically ill but those who are really needed his work, really benefited from it). Whatever the arguments of treatment versus culture, Bernard Rimland certainly celebrated the personhood of his son, a creative man in his own right, but also had the clarity to care about the often serious medical challenges of those with autism who dealt with serious health problems.

Wherever you are "Bernie," shine on.²

■　　■　　■　　■　　■　　■　　■　　■　　■　　■

the room numbers and made a flow chart from one class to another. Because of his difficulty in getting around, the first week of school he was late for every class.

Jack Donehey-Nykiel is a young man majoring in Islamic Studies in college. Jack was diagnosed with Asperger's syndrome when he was thirteen and has challenges in the area of orientation mobility and used to get lost a lot before he learned how to ask for help.

Oral Hyposensitivity

Nick Dubin, author of *Asperger Syndrome and Bullying: Strategies and Solutions*, was diagnosed at age twenty-seven and has a master's degree in special education. Nick reports having such good motor skills that he was a very good and valued tennis player on the high school tennis team. Yet his fine motor skills were so behind that, even as a teen, he could not tie his shoelaces. Nick also remembers clearly being orally hyposensitive, meaning his mouth needed a great deal of oral stimulation. For this reason, Nick would put foreign objects in his mouth, chew them, and then swallow them. In medical terminology, this behavior is called "pica." Obviously, for safety reasons, among others, his pica was of huge concern to everyone. To this day, he catches himself still having the urge to put foreign objects in his mouth, but as he puts it: "Fortunately, chewing gum was invented to satisfy that urge. The key is not to swallow the chewing gum!"

At the other extreme, many children find having their teeth brushed to be painful because of oral hypersensitivity. Occupational therapists

FOOD FOR THOUGHT

SENSORY QUOTA SYSTEM: AN ILLUSTRATION

Say my brain has only 100 Sensory Processing Units. If it takes 95 units to decipher the sounds of a conversation, translate the conversational signals such as innuendos, pick up the contextual clues that impart social meaning, and modulate my voice, I have just five units remaining for other sensory sources. Since looking at someone's face, decoding facial expressions, and coping with the pain of the fluorescent lights requires (hypothetically) at least 75 units, in this case I would not have enough Sensory Processing Units to look at the other person, or even open my eyes, while we conversed. This helps explain why most autistic people are unable to look at someone in the eyes while also talking, a characteristic behavior of autism spectrum disorders.

—Zosia Zaks, *Life and Love:
Positive Strategies for Autistic Adults* [3]

have some suggestions for desensitizing the mouth, including rubbing the gums gently with a soft washcloth.

Nick describes how receiving the Asperger's diagnosis at twenty-seven was the most liberating moment of his life, as it allowed him to understand the underpinnings of his neurological wiring in a way that therapy and psychology had been unable to do.

How Challenges with Sensory Processing Can Lead to Sensory Overload

After learning more about all the difficulties people on the spectrum are confronted with on a daily basis because of processing issues, it is no wonder they often experience sensory and emotional overload. Many adults on the spectrum experienced this as a child and still do today, but many have learned how to overcome or deal with this challenge, or experience it at a lesser intensity.

When I met Zosia Zaks, author of *Life and Love: Positive Strategies for Autistic Adults*, she was wearing dark glasses because her eyes were sensitive to the light in the hotel lobby where we met. It was an ongoing series of vocational problems that led Zosia to be diagnosed at the age of thirty-one. When she was a child, it was suggested to her parents (by both an educator and a psychiatrist) that Zosia might be autistic, but at the time her parents did not think so because she could talk. Zosia shared with me how being diagnosed as an adult helped her to understand the difficulties she had experienced. In her book, she uses the illustration of having a Sensory Quota System in the brain to explain how sensory overload works (see "Food for Thought," page 18). Zosia's description makes clear how taxing it can be for children on the spectrum when they are trying to learn academics in our typical school environments as well as trying to understand all the social aspects.

Why Transitions Can Be So Difficult

If a child is oversensitive to light, sound, touch, and other senses, it makes him anxious about when he will next be bombarded by too much stimuli. This is why some children with autism resist change: they are fearful of the unknown. Any change in routine could mean they will be bombarded by sensory stimuli that they haven't anticipated and can't prepare for, which leads them to feel anxious and fearful, putting them in emotional as well as sensory overload.

For example, my son, Jeremy, always hated going to the haircutter and going to the dentist because the top of his head and his mouth are sensitive areas, and because he does not like the buzzing noises that go along with the tools they use. When he was little, I used to have a daily schedule with picture icons that I would show him as I verbally explained to him the schedule for the day. For a visit to the dentist or haircutter, I would put a weekly schedule up and show him a few days before and remind him every day as well as the morning of the visit that we would be going after school. It was difficult for him but he tolerated it, looking very relieved when it was over. At the time, I had no idea how little or how much Jeremy understood, but evidently he made the connection because if I forgot to put it on the schedule and to tell him in advance, I could get him in the car to go, but once we arrived, I could not get him out of the car. It seems he was preparing himself mentally to go when he had the advance notice.

Brian King explains that he doesn't like surprises because he can't assimilate information fast enough to take it all in. Because of this, big surprises can make him very anxious—for example, if his boss asks him to do something right away, without advance notice. Brian explains that new things cause him to freeze for a bit while he transitions and he tries not to panic. The more time he has to adjust to the change, the better he is able to deal with it. Counting things such as how many chairs are in the room or how many buttons are on someone's shirt helps him become more secure in an unfamiliar situation.

Jordan Ackerson is the son of Lisa Lieberman, author of *A Stranger Among Us: Hiring In-Home Support for a Child with Autism Spectrum Disorders and Other Neurological Differences*. Jordan graduated in 2007 with a modified high school diploma and attends a community college. When asked whether sensory or emotional overload continues to be a factor for him, he says that sudden sounds can make him feel "caught off-guard."

Emotionally, Jordan says that it takes him a long time to process and let go of internal emotional reactions. He feels overwhelmed when he has random racing thoughts about one thing or another. His mother states that providing Jordan with the opportunity to have a one-on-one relationship with a child therapist who could understand his unique needs as a person with autism has been very helpful in guiding him to develop coping skills.

Children and others on the spectrum do have emotions. As Amanda Baggs explains, they do not always show them in the same way neurotypicals do. Some autistic people describe their emotions as arising in different situations than most people, but they all have them in one form or another, and some on the spectrum have far more emotions than most people are aware of. Understanding the sensory aspects of their emotional responses is a great step toward helping them cope with new situations and experiences.

PRACTICAL TIP

Taking pictures or videos of new places and people and explaining them to your child before he goes to a new environment can be helpful for difficulties with transitions—whether the challenge is one of orientation mobility, transitioning to new environments, and or anxiety. This helps with understanding and preparing for changes. Taking a child to a new school and walking around when it is empty before he attends it is also a positive strategy.

Fear and Anxiety

Temple Grandin's professional training as an animal scientist and her history as a person with autism have given her a unique perspective on both human and animal behavior. Temple says that autistic people can often think the way animals think. In *Animals in Translation: Using the Mysteries of Autism to Decode Animal Behavior*, she discusses how fear is the main emotion in autism and is a dreadful problem for many. Anxiety also plays a major part in the lives of many on the spectrum. Temple defines fear as a response to external threats and anxiety as a response to internal threats. Looking at sensory overload, it is easy to see how the external threat of sensory bombardments can cause people on the spectrum to feel fearful. It also makes sense that a person on the spectrum with highly sensitive processing would be prone to being anxious and feeling emotional overload.

Temple experienced constant fear and anxiety and panic attacks upon reaching puberty. She invented the "squeeze machine" for herself after observing animals at her aunt's ranch in a cattle squeeze chute where they would place animals for their vaccinations. She saw how calm the animals appeared, so she put herself in the chute, and it had a very calming effect on her.

It is important to recognize that sensory and emotional overload can actually produce physical changes in the person. Think about how you feel immediately following a narrowly missed car crash or after drinking

▦   ▦   F O O D   F O R   T H O U G H T   ▦   ▦

HOW DEALING WITH NEW SITUATIONS CAN BE DIFFICULT

Brian King, LCSW, is a licensed clinical social worker and autism consultant. On his informative website, www.ImAnAspie.com, he explains how he deals with new situations:

When entering into situations I can't control (which is often) I do a lot of rehearsal beforehand. When meeting new people I run through the do's and don'ts in my head and decide a few things I'm going to do to start things off (such as a hello and a handshake) and then let the other person take the lead whenever possible. Springing unexpected things on me that require an immediate change in direction often causes me to freeze for a bit while I transition and try not to panic. The more time I have to adjust to the change the better I'm able to deal with it. I find I'm more secure in an unfamiliar environment by counting things in the room. How many chairs, how many buttons on someone's shirt. Even numbers are best because it cognitively gives me a sense of evenness and balance. I usually do this when I first walk into a new place or have to sit and wait for a while, especially when I don't know how long I'll be waiting. I'll do it over and over until I feel calm.[4]

▦   ▦   ▦   ▦   ▦   ▦   ▦   ▦   ▦   ▦

five double espressos: your body is racing, you can feel your heart beating very quickly. This is why in some self-regulation techniques, children and teens on the spectrum are taught to think about how fast their engine is running on a scale of 1 to 5, or how high their emotions are between 1 and 5, and eventually what activities to practice to get to a 3, which is optimal (self-regulation is discussed at length in Chapter 6).

Amanda Baggs explains that she had to learn over the years how to deal with sensory overload. She realized that anything her body chose to do in response to overload (unless it was harmful to herself or to others) was probably what needed to happen. She discovered that if she let go of trying to keep her body still in one spot, then it would usually move around in a way that would drastically reduce her overload and increase her comprehension level. Others have discussed how they needed to flap and jump to keep self-regulated. This could explain some of the behaviors you see in your child. Self-regulation is another essential skill, and this will be discussed in Chapter 6.

Kamran Nazeer, a successful British government policy advisor and author of *Send in the Idiots: Stories from the Other Side of Autism*, shared with me that as a child he remembers that he would often rock back and forth, probably as a response to sensory overload. As an adult, he still feels the need to retreat to something basic in a desire for internal cohesion. Kamran's sensory overload has lessened over time and the technique he uses to deal with it has changed. He has learned to use inconspicuous techniques; now he can simply touch and feel the texture of his trousers under his fingers.

Problems of Connection, Control, and Tolerance

Donna Williams believes that the three recognized traits of autism (impairments in social interaction, communication disorder, and obsessive behaviors) are in fact problems of connection, control, and tolerance. In her book *Autism: An Inside-Out Approach*, Donna describes connection as being about making sense of the world. If a child is unable to make sense of the world around him, then he will have problems with responding with intention to his environment or to the people around him, meaning he will have a problem of control, leading to obsessive behaviors, compulsions, and acute anxiety. Being unable to make sense of the world also means having problems of tolerance, or being able to stand the world or oneself, meaning sensory and emotional hypersensitivity.

Donna also describes meaning deafness, meaning blindness, lack of body connectedness, and lacking simultaneous processing of a sense of self and other as challenges to children on the spectrum. In recent years, Donna has discussed these traits as being like agnosia, where there is a loss of ability to recognize objects, persons, sounds, shapes, or smells while the specific sense is not defective nor is there any significant memory loss. If a child is experiencing many of these processing difficulties, it can be he is living in constant sensory overload. This means we really need to explain everything to children on the spectrum, help them make connections and prepare for what is coming next, by using the sensory channel that appears to be working best for them.

Sensory overload can also affect the acquisition of such basic functional skills as being toilet trained, which is a real challenge for parents of children on the spectrum. Some children learn relatively easily and quickly, but most do not. Because of the difficulties experienced by my son, this topic is of particular interest to me (I never dreamed I would still be discussing toileting issues when both my children are teens, but I digress). I used behavioral techniques for many years to help my son in this area. However, I noticed that when he stayed out in the sun or entered stores with bright fluorescent lighting, he would wet himself. When he was going through difficult times emotionally, he would also have toileting accidents. It was not until he could spell out what was going on that he could tell me that he can't "feel" his body when the light is too bright or in moments of emotional duress.

I was surprised to learn, quite by accident, that many adults on the more able end of the spectrum still have challenges in this area as well. As mentioned earlier in this chapter, Donna Williams has difficulties differentiating between a full bladder and a hungry stomach. Other adults shared similar stories. One person I interviewed told me she has these difficulties particularly in sensory overload situations such as crowded, noisy, brightly lit hotel lobbies or conference centers. My curiosity was piqued, and in asking more adults, I found that some set alarms on their pagers or cell phones to remind them to use the toilet at certain intervals. Besides the sensory overload, there is the risk of having to wait too long in line and being in an unfamiliar stall with the toilet paper in a different spot than they are used to: all this is quite taxing when you are on the edge of sensory overload.

The interesting aspect about all this for me was that for years the behaviorists would scratch their heads when looking at my son, because they could not figure out why Jeremy was still having "wetting accidents" although we were doing all these behavior plans. Toilet training difficulties always seem to be associated with low intelligence or "low functioning," and yet this appears not to be the case.

PRACTICAL TIP

It is very important to try to figure out what kind of learner your child or student is—auditory, tactile, visual, or a bit of all three. Look at how he interacts with his environment and with tabletop tasks you give him. Does he readily put together more and more complicated puzzles? Does he have trouble progressing from one puzzle to a new one? If his motor function is working, it could be he has problems "seeing" the puzzle. Using only visual techniques to teach this child may not be effective. Does the child repeat bits of dialogue heard on television or sing songs? Try pairing visual supports and basic verbal instruction. Sometimes singing will help teach the sequencing of simple steps, for example, "This is the way we wash our hands . . . " Does the child "feel" his way around the room, touching the walls and bumping into furniture? Teaching with the use of tactile materials may be helpful.

All that being said, I strongly recommend behavioral approaches to toilet training if you are encountering difficulties. They were and still are very helpful for training Jeremy to control his body and to use the restroom appropriately. I would suggest that if you see patterns of wetting accidents, you take data on environmental factors (light, noise, etc.) because this will help you devise some strategies for your child to learn to self-regulate in this problem area.

How Sensory Processing Affects Learning

It is often stated that children with autism are visual learners. It is true that many are, but not everyone is. Many times when our children fail to learn, it is because we are not using the sensory channel that is their strongest. Rather than assuming a child is not capable of understanding and learning, we should try to figure out which sensory channel is the best learning channel for the child and use a teaching method adapted to that.

For example, a child who likes looking at books may appear to be visually processing information, while he might really just be staring at one particular spot, letter, or detail in a picture, and not processing the information. It is important to figure out if the child is using his visual processing for learning or for stimming.

Temple Grandin, as mentioned earlier in this chapter, is a visual learner. She thinks in pictures, meaning if she hears the word "church," many pictures of specific churches she has seen in the past come to mind.

Brian King is also a very logical, concrete, and visual thinker. He associates images with much of what's being said to him. Brian feels this enables him to think more quickly and creatively since he has so much more information to work with compared to a person who thinks only in words. Brian sees the words and the pictures. He finds the thinking of other people fascinating as well as the words they use to describe their thinking. This is what allows him to appear personable and social. He likes to listen to people assemble their thoughts and explain why they think as they do. Brian feels that his ability to deconstruct and rearrange thinking into different perceptions is his greatest Asperger's gift, and he likens it to rewriting computer code to make the computer do something different.

Donna Williams, however, is not a visual thinker. She describes herself as a kinesthetic thinker, a systems thinker, a musical thinker. She describes her world as being a physical and sensory one of pattern, theme, and feel, her mind like a mosaic, her conscious thoughts intangible until she experiences them after they've been expressed—usually through the arts. Because of her fragmented vision and meaning blindness, she learns kinesthetically, through direct physical experience and hands-on doing.

Besides taking into consideration a child's best learning channel, taking a look at the environment to make sure it is not too overwhelming to the child is essential. Temple Grandin often talks about how the classrooms in the 1950s when she was a child were quiet and they had minimal distractions on the wall, so a child could more easily focus. For a child on the spectrum who feels things much more intensely, it can be very difficult to process anything indeed in our current elementary school classrooms that are awash with sensory distractions.

■   ■   F O O D   F O R   T H O U G H T   ■   ■

THE CONNECTION BETWEEN LEARNING AND THE ENVIRONMENT

As teaching is taking place, parents and teachers can sometimes become so intent on immersing their kids in social situations that they underestimate—or forget about—the impact that sensory issues have on a child's ability to learn social skills and develop social awareness. When sensory and social overlap, social learning won't take place. It can't because the sensory issues are interfering with the child's ability to attend and learn. The anxiety over sensory issues can be acute and can completely fill the child's field of awareness. . . . That's why anyone trying to teach social skills—even basic ones—to a child with ASD needs to first assess the environment from a sensory perspective and eliminate sensory issues that will impede the child's ability to concentrate on the social lesson. . . . parents and teachers scratch their heads and wonder why the child can't learn basic social skills or isn't interested in even trying? What do they expect when the child is put in an environment that hurts? Fluorescent lights may be flickering like a disco-dance floor, and the sound they make may feel like a dentist drill hitting a nerve. Could you learn under those conditions?

—Temple Grandin, *Unwritten Rules of Social Relationships: Decoding Social Mysteries Through the Unique Perspectives of Autism.*[5]

■   ■   ■   ■   ■   ■   ■   ■   ■   ■

Conclusion

If a child does not appear to understand what you are trying to teach him, do not assume mental retardation. Assume major challenges with sensory processing. In order to help a child learn, figure which sensory channel appears to be working the best and adapt your teaching methods. People who have overcome sensory processing challenges have used a variety of methods: biomedical interventions, diets, behavior modification, desensitization, sensory integration, occupational therapy, auditory training, special lenses, vision therapy, and so on. Methods used successfully depend on the intensity of the processing challenge, what it stems from, and the individual child. There is not one "right" therapy or strategy; parents must learn to look at their child and analyze the difficulties and abilities to determine which therapies could prove effective. Consulting with an occupational therapist who is trained in sensory integration is extremely helpful. A knowledgeable professional can provide therapy and make suggestions for how to help desensitize your child throughout his or her day.

2

Communication

He wants to learn, and speaking as a teacher, that is the key to success. Due to his disability, he might have "speed bumps" throughout his life which deter the zeal, but explaining his thoughts in writing and conversation have really helped him through those rough periods.

—Allan Gustafson, interview with Jeremy Sicile-Kira, spring 2007

Autism is an important influence in my life. The hardest part is not being able to talk. God must have been out of voices when he made me.

Some good people have been important to my success in communicating. An Indian woman, Soma, was the most important person to make people understand that I was able to learn. My mother asked the school to try to teach me like Soma did. Maureen and Allan are great teachers. Some other helpful people have been my "Afternoon Angels."

—Jeremy Sicile-Kira,
paper for sociology class, March 2006

As a baby and toddler, my son, Jeremy, did not have much in the way of communication skills. I would have had to have been a behavior expert or a person with autism to understand the little he did communicate, but at the time I was neither. Even at mealtimes at home in Paris, although he loved to eat, he never pointed to or grabbed the food or drink items he wanted. He never took my hand to show what he wanted. He just waited.

We worked hard at trying to establish a method of communication. I tried FC (facilitated communication) when he was about four, just to get him to point to objects and pictures and words with some success, although we did not do it long enough to work on the independence part. I was just trying to get him to understand that he could make a choice. I did teach him to spell out some words from a French picture dictionary, and he loved doing that.

Then we started a behaviorally based home program, in the United Kingdom, where we were living at the time, one of the first families there to do so. Jeremy learned to say and use more than 100 words in a natural environment. He would walk into the kitchen and say "cheese" when he wanted a snack or go to the front door and say "car" when he wanted to go for a ride.

When we moved back to the United States, he was still stuck at the one-word level of communication, so we tried using the Picture Exchange Communication System (PECS). This was good because he could pick a picture icon and put it on the "I want . . . " sentence strip. Before long, Jeremy was verbally saying "I want . . . " and he could now string three words together. However, he had a hard time opening his PECS book, finding the right picture, and putting it on the sentence strip. For years we used a combination of PECS and verbal sentences, but he never progressed past the three-word "I want . . . " sentence, although he did learn the verbal labels for new favorite items.

Then, when he was in junior high, I heard about Soma Mukhopadhyay and her son, Tito, and the RPM (Rapid Prompting Method; see "Food for Thought," page 32) she had developed to teach him and was now using in a classroom of autistic children in Los Angeles, through the auspices of the Cure Autism Now Foundation. I went to the classroom and observed Soma. Afterward, I tried to work with my son, but I wasn't really sure what to do.

Eventually, I started taking Jeremy to Soma's twice a month, and over two years' time I learned how to work with Jeremy, who was progressing academically. I was concerned about the lack of research and possible inadvertent prompting I might be doing (unlike FC, no one is giving physical support to the arm of the child; however, with Jeremy, we were still holding the letterboard or litewriter because of his visual processing and eye-hand coordination challenges). However, after they started using RPM at school, we had ample opportunities to validate that RPM was an effective teaching strategy for Jeremy and that he was accurately relaying information to different tutors and at home.

Jeremy's success in finding a way to communicate was not a miracle; it was the result of a lot of hard work on everyone's part. Jeremy still has a long way to go in order to be more fluent on the litewriter and transfer his skills to the computer, but for now we are encouraging communication with as many different people as possible.

The Importance of Communication

After making sense of the world around us, communication is the most important and primal of abilities. Children on the spectrum need to be able to communicate in order to get their needs met—as do all children. Granted, not everyone has to be an eloquent speaker and a great letter writer, but we all need to be able to ask for what we want, to tell someone how we feel, to ask for help, and to share vital information. Communication difficulties for adults on the spectrum can range from being nonverbal and having practically no system of communication, to someone who can be an eloquent speaker or writer yet may miss out on the subtleties of body language. Some who have adequate verbal skills may be missing out on the meaning of metaphors and or on knowing how to start and end a conversation.

Imagine not being able to tell someone what you are thinking

▦ ▦ FOOD FOR THOUGHT ▦ ▦

IMPROVING ACADEMIC SUCCESS AND COMMUNICATION

Soma Mukhopadhyay developed the Rapid Prompting Method (RPM) to teach her own son, Tito, who is a published writer despite his autism. Soma is the educational director of Helping Autism Through Learning and Outreach (HALO), a nonprofit organization that provides RPM instruction in its Austin, Texas, clinic. RPM is instruction for improving academic success leading toward communication for persons with autism and similar challenges. The following is information from their website at www.halo-soma.org:

RPM (Rapid Prompting Method) is used to teach academics, and communication is also taught in the process. Despite behaviors, the academic focus of every RPM lesson is designed to activate the reasoning part of the brain so that the student becomes distracted by and engaged in learning.

RPM uses a "Teach-Ask" paradigm for eliciting responses through intensive verbal, auditory, visual and/or tactile prompts. RPM presumes competence to increase students' interest, confidence and self-esteem. Prompting competes with each student's self-stimulatory behavior, and is designed to help students initiate a response. Student responses evolve from picking up answers, to pointing, to typing and writing which reveals students' comprehension, academic abilities and eventually, conversational skills. RPM is a low-tech approach in that it requires only an instructor, student, paper and pencil. But the science behind how and why it works for some individuals is much more complex.

For most people, listening to information, understanding it, preparing a response and utilizing the necessary muscles to communicate that response is a subconscious, reflexive process. But for someone with severe autism, this same process can be a convoluted task. We know from what Tito (Soma's son and published author) and others with autism have communicated that it is extremely difficult to process the sensory information with which they easily become overloaded. Thus, to focus on hearing and seeing, to formulate an appropriate response, and then to complete the motor planning necessary to give that response requires tremendous effort and initiative. Thanks to scientists and people with autism who have participated in research, we are beginning to understand the brain functions of a person with autism, how all the different areas work (or don't work) together

*and how other parts of the brain can be trained to provide support for the parts that
are not working properly.*

*Although future research is anticipated, neuroscientists such as Dr. Michael
Merzenich, PhD, a professor at the University of California San Francisco and a
researcher at the W. M. Keck Center for Integrative Neuroscience, have affirmed
that Soma's teaching method will benefit many of the children and adults with
autism who struggle daily to learn, function and communicate in traditional academic settings.*

and feeling or constantly being misunderstood. Imagine trying to tell
your mom what you want for breakfast and only the same echolalic
phrase keeps coming out of your mouth despite your efforts to say the
right words. Imagine feeling sick, or getting hurt at school, and having
no way to tell your parents. Imagine people judging you as retarded
because you can't communicate as others do, and because you behave a bit
strangely.

Imagine that as a child you have pretty good verbal skills, but you
can understand only the literal meanings of words and sentences, and so
you are at a loss to comprehend some of what is going on. Imagine not
knowing the "hidden curriculum"—those social rules and understood
norms that people just seem to pick up by osmosis, but about which you
haven't a clue. Imagine your behaviors being misunderstood because you
don't use the same kind of body language as nonautistic people. These are
just some of the communication difficulties experienced, to different
degrees, by children on the spectrum.

Nonverbal Children: The Need to Find an Appropriate Communication System

Despite the recognized importance of communication, there are many
children on the spectrum who grow up to become adults with very
limited means of communication. There are many reasons for this.

First and foremost, if you have read the previous chapter, you will have understood how difficult it is for a person with sensory processing challenges to be able to get all the processes working together to form viable communication.

Second, children with autism are often misjudged by their erratic behavior (usually caused by sensory processing challenges in environments that are hard for them to handle), the way they look, and their inability to respond to the teaching methods (often visual) we are imposing on them. We assume that if a method worked for some or many children, it should work for all. Therefore, we conclude that most autistic children must be retarded. However, adults such as Sue Rubin (writer and subject of the documentary *Autism Is a World*), Amanda Baggs, Tito Mukhopadhyay, Jeremy, and many others have shown that, despite prejudice and misconception, they are capable of learning and are able to communicate. This makes me wonder how many other people out there are really capable of much more than we give them credit for. I find it hard to believe that the people mentioned above are as rare as some seem to believe.

Third, parents and professionals working with nonverbal young children on the spectrum are often hesitant to try alternative forms of communication other than speech, as they are afraid it will keep the child from learning to speak. However, research shows us that alternative forms of communication—whether sign language, a picture symbol system, a text-based communication device, or another approach—can actually help a child develop speech. Often the alternative form of communication creates a needed bridge for speech to develop. And if the child does not develop speech, at least he will have a way to communicate.

Finally, many people are suspicious of methods such as facilitated communication and the Rapid Prompting Method, which defy the stereotypes that have existed for decades about the perceived mental retardation of nonverbal people. In addition, the first research studies done on FC were unable to validate that the facilitators were not the ones initiating the communication. Moreover, independence was not taught from the beginning as it is now. However, even Dr. Bernard Rimland, who was staunchly opposed to facilitated communication, suggested cer-

PRACTICAL TIP

Reading to your child every day is important, even if she does not appear to be understanding. First of all, that one-on-one connection is precious for any child. Second, she will be getting used to listening to your voice and the sound of speech, and eventually connect the words with the illustrations or written words in the book. Giving young children access to picture books with words clearly labeling objects is great as a basic starter. Children who learned to type did not just one day learn how to spell and put sentences together; they gained literacy skills over time through what they heard and saw.

If your child is nonverbal, find a good speech therapist who understands autism and is knowledgeable about the different types of alternative communication systems available, and who is knowledgeable about augmentative communication systems and assistive technology.

tain simple tests parents could try at home with their child, and was open to the fact that, on a case-by-case basis, it could be valid. Thanks to more recent research that has been favorable to the validity of FC, and to the fact that more adults on the spectrum have reached independence, there is now more acceptance of this method.

Although more research is needed on both RPM and FC, I would suggest that parents and teachers of nonverbal autistic children who have problems with motor planning and sensory processing as well as no viable means of communication look into both these methods to see if they can be helpful. The important thing is to determine what makes sense for your child and to strive to teach independence as soon as possible (for example, when using FC, decreasing the hold and eventually going to no hold). It is important to get proper training in any method you use. There are ways to validate on a case-by-case basis that true communication is occurring and that it is not being prompted by the support person. At any rate, if you have a child whom no one has been able to provide with a way of communicating, what have you got to lose?

If a child is not taught an effective means of communication, he will

NONCOMPLIANCE MAY BE COMMUNICATING BOREDOM

Mr. Gustafson, case manager, has known Jeremy Sicile-Kira for seven months. The first two months, Mr. Gustafson was frustrated by the goals for Jeremy. For the most part, it was Jeremy's behavior (defiance and disinterest) in activities in the class-room. After talking with the mother, she said Jeremy does more difficult tasks at home and does well. She used a method called RPM (the Rapid Prompting Method) to have Jeremy engage in the learning process. After two months assess-ing Jeremy's grade level, Mr. Gustafson found out that Jeremy could handle fifth grade curriculum and that sixth grade curriculum would be the best target for teaching. . . . . The implementation of the new goals has had a positive effect on Jeremy's attitude in class. Jeremy used to knock work out of my hands and move around agitated in his seat during lessons, but since the level of work has become more difficult, the level of inappropriate behavior has gone down during lesson time. In two months, Jeremy has already succeeded in passing some of the goals made in January.

—Allan Gustafson, teacher, Individualized Educational Program (IEP)
Team meeting notes, March 30, 2005

learn to communicate through his behavior. This may not always be pleasant to those around him, and it certainly will limit what the child can communicate about. A child who tantrums or is aggressive is trying to communicate, but we are not always able to figure out what the child is communicating (hunger, scratchy clothes, anger, sickness). This kind of communicative behavior may keep the child from participating in a society that is not always so forgiving of differences. All children need to be taught a way of communicating their needs, wants, and pains, and hopefully even to carry on conversations so that we can know what they are thinking and help them as they grow into adults.

Nonverbal adults or teens who have learned to type say it is impor-tant to them that they feel confidence and respect from the person teaching them. DJ Savarese, who wrote the last chapter in his father's book, *Reasonable People: A Memoir of Autism and Adoption*, says that "treated as human and deserving respect and choices" are the most important factors of learning how to communicate. When asked how he learned to communicate, DJ replies, "I used pictures and signs. Then learned to read and write so I could seriously type everything I hoped to say, I boldly freed my responses both caring to join people and folding fear." DJ had a difficult childhood before being adopted by Ralph and Emily Savarese. Emily was an inclusions specialist and had experience with autism before adopting DJ. She has devoted most of her time to helping him become the person he is today, academically successful and a capable communicator.

Why Do Many Verbal Children Have Problems with Communication?

There are different ways in which verbal children have difficulties. Many times, children on the spectrum may be verbal but they are not really communicating. Often they will repeat snippets of dialogue heard on the television. Temple Grandin often says that this form of echolalia is a good sign that the child has some capacity to learn speech. It could be because they have gotten familiar with that voice, if they watch a video over and over, and so they can decipher the sounds. Once a child is repeating a phrase, it is a good idea to attach meaning or sense to it. Sometimes, Jeremy has delayed echolalia, which means he repeats a phrase or words previously heard at home, but at another time in appropriate circumstances. For example, if he slips going down the stairs, he will say, "Whoops, be careful," because he has heard me say that in a similar situation.

There are many on the more functionally able end of the spectrum who are very articulate but still have trouble with aspects of neurotypical conversation. For example, many are literal thinkers and do not understand metaphors, or have problems with the "hidden curriculum," which are things we take for granted that those on the spectrum do not. For example, a teacher may tell her class to "Put a lid on it!" meaning to

---

PRACTICAL TIP

To help your child or student, teach him whenever the opportunity arises about the "hidden curriculum." If you think about what it is like for a foreigner trying to learn our expressions and customs, you will appreciate your child's difficulty in this arena a bit more. Giving him a clear explanation of what an expression means and when it is appropriate to use it will make life much easier for him.

---

quiet down, and a student with very literal thinking will not understand this. Until it is explained to him what that expression means, he will focus on finding a lid. These types of difficulties affect social relationships and how people on the spectrum respond. A child may be invited for a sleepover and assume she will be getting her normal amount of sleep, not knowing that slumber parties usually entail very little sleep at all.

Although we often think of people on the spectrum as having communicating difficulties, it is interesting to note that some are very articulate despite being on the spectrum and actually earn a living using language. Michael John Carley spent many years as a playwright and then was a diplomat in the Middle East. He once told me that being a diplomat was interesting and the communication aspects were not difficult because there are very specific rules of communication and hierarchy in diplomacy that everyone must follow. Sean Barron, who coauthored *Unwritten Rules of Social Relationships: Decoding Social Mysteries Through the Unique Perspective of Autism* with Temple Grandin, is a journalist. Kamran Nazeer, author of *Send in the Idiots*, is a policy maker in the United Kingdom. In his book, Kamran talks about two of his classmates, both of whom are also on the spectrum: one is a speechwriter for the Democratic Party, and the other uses puppets to communicate with others. Kamran describes how the complexity of language is helpful for someone like him, because he can follow rules; it is having to rely on the nuances that make understanding more difficult.

People with Asperger's and on the more functionally able end of the spectrum also tend to have trouble reading body language, understanding what a nonautistic person is conveying by the expressions on their face, their posture, and so on. The subtleties are very hard for them to grasp. Ruth Elaine Joyner Hane is active with the Autism Society of America (ASA) on a national level and was diagnosed with autism as an adult in 1995. She is also a consultant to individuals with health challenges. Ruth contributed a chapter to Stephen Shore's book *Ask and Tell*, titled "Communicating Through Advocacy and Self-Disclosure: Four Ways to Connect." In it, she discusses the difficulties that can occur when we talk and the sender (talker) or the receiver (listener) has a problem picking up or "reading" the signals. This loss of connection often happens when a nonautistic person and someone on the spectrum are trying to have a conversation. Ruth suggests that we need to send clear signals and become more aware of our reliance on body language, among other nonverbal cues. She gives ideas on how people on the spectrum can learn to read faces and read body posture, as these are areas that are of particular trouble.

When I call Brian King to interview him, he speaks to me in a formal and precise manner. Although some people with Asperger's syndrome typically have a flat monotone voice, this is not true for him. Brian reports having studied public speaking extensively and has learned how to vary his voice effectively to get his points across. He also shares that one of his Aspie gifts is the ability to remember sounds and voices the way he heard them, which has given him a flair for speaking with a number of accents. Brian enjoys public speaking because he can talk about a topic he is interested in and can look briefly at people in the audience without the need for extended eye contact. However, he makes it clear that he finds "fluff talk" (phrases that neurotypicals use out of habit, without much meaning, such as "Good morning" or "How are you?") presumptuous and irrelevant, and he refrains from using them. Brian feels anxious if people ask him how he is doing, because he feels compelled to stop and actually assess himself in order to give an honest response. Others have mentioned to me that they have difficulty with

■   ■   FOOD FOR THOUGHT   ■   ■

WHAT'S MANAGEABLE IN LANGUAGE

However, it isn't the complexity of language, the array of suffixes, or the prolifera-tion of rules for making plurals that causes difficulty for autistic individuals. In fact, the complexity probably helps. . . . The more rules and structures there are, the less an autistic individual has to rely on intuition and context to get the meaning of someone else's utterance. One meaning, one word would be the ideal. That's manageable.

—Kamran Nazeer, *Send in the Idiots: Stories from the Other Side of Autism.*[6]

■   ■   ■   ■   ■   ■   ■   ■   ■   ■

"small talk" or idle chitchat. People on the spectrum do not understand why it's necessary or useful.

All these challenges can be compared to the experience of visiting a foreign country. Whether or not you are familiar with the language spoken there, you probably will not understand the subtleties of the culture, the idioms, and so on. People with autism have to learn these subtleties. For example, when I moved to France after college, I was fluent in French because of having been raised bilingual in America by my French parents, but I had my American manners. One day after living there a few months, I was corrected by my cousin, who told me I had to stop saying "thank you" when someone gave me a compliment, as this was considered rude (i.e., you are acknowledging that you know how good you are) and that instead you are supposed to say, "Do you think so?" People knew I had been raised in America, so they understood my cultural gaffe. People on the spectrum, even those on the more able end of it, are usually not afforded the same leeway, as their disability is not as readily recognized or understood.

The Connection Between Behavior and Communication

As mentioned earlier, behavior is a form of communication. Often, we focus too much on stopping behavior and redirecting it without figuring out what the intended *purpose* of the behavior might be. We all need to learn appropriate behavior. But more important, we need to have a form of communication we can ably and comfortably use to express ourselves. Sue Rubin is a nonverbal autistic woman and successful student at Whittier College. Sue learned to type by using facilitated communication and has been mainstreamed since her high school years. She wrote the screenplay for and starred in *Autism Is a World*, a documentary that was nominated for an Academy Award. As Sue explained in her presentation at the Autism Society of America's national conference in 2007, it was learning a form of communication that enabled her to take more control over her behavior (see "Food for Thought," later in this chapter). Although she still needs a reinforcement program, Sue explains that learning a form of communication allowed the logical part of her brain to take over.

My son, Jeremy, had some basic communication systems over the years before learning to spell on a letterboard; however, he also had some behaviors that clearly were communication though the meaning was not always easily apparent. When the television was on or guests were over for dinner, he would leave the room and go to the upstairs balcony. I could see him there, standing and rocking. It took me a while to figure out he did this when noise levels were too high. When we would switch to a quieter program on low volume, when guests were few, or when there was a lull in the conversation, he would come back downstairs.

Another behavior that perplexed me years ago was that he would remove all the books off the bookshelves and put them on the floor. No amount of behavioral intervention helped; he just learned to empty the shelves when we weren't looking. He didn't mind having to put them all back. Recently he started pulling down all the autism books I have collected over the years whenever he could. This time I could ask him why he was doing it. He replied that he wanted me to read him a book about autism—about someone like him—and he was looking for the right book. Now, I occasionally read to him from various books on the shelves, and he no longer pulls them down.

The Importance of Communicating with Autistic Peers

Blogger and advocate Amanda Baggs reports that communication was complicated for her as she learned about it in bits and pieces. When she could talk at what she calls her most "normal appearing," she would chatter on about her favorite topics, but there were a lot of things she could not say. Because of her movement disorder and other difficulties, she would only partly learn some aspects of communication, then forget and relearn them, and so on. It was contact with autistic people who used language that was the most important factor to learning communication with any permanence. Amanda says it is because they used communication to discuss experiences they had in common, and this helped her describe the way she saw the world in general, using words that she knew were the right ones to describe her experience.

Amanda was nine years old when she started to learn how to type. She learned using a typing tutor program on the computers at her school. The program featured a cat, which made her automatically interested. Amanda points out that some people need more physical assistance learning typing than she did, and others might need assistance developing the literacy skills required to communicate through writing. Others might need an alternate form of communication altogether.

Amanda believes that autistic and nonautistic people perceive different kinds and amounts of information about the world around us, and then respond differently to the information they perceive. Because much of the information perceived by autistic people is not perceived by nonautistic people at all, many of their responses to their environment are incomprehensible to nonautistic people.

Amanda quotes Donna Williams, who once said that "normal is being in the company of those like yourself." For Amanda, being around other autistic people, particularly the ones she "clicks" with, can feel like

---

PRACTICAL TIP

Finding peers—on or off the spectrum—is not always easy. Sometimes there are classmates, neighbors, children at your place of worship, or friends of siblings who can provide friendship or companionship and become peer buddies and mentors. Many middle schools and high schools have "Best Buddy" programs. Peer training can be helpful; indeed, for those more impacted by autism or communication difficulties, some form of peer training is necessary for any communication to take place.

---

being normal. She finds it amazing how they communicate so well among themselves yet "our conversations with nonautistic people are fraught with extremes of misinterpretation in both directions."

However, Amanda does not want to imply that there is only one kind of autistic communication. There are autistic people Amanda communicates easily with and autistic people whose communication is alien and overloading to her. This is why she feels it is crucial to be exposed to a variety of peers.

Amanda has written that some of the bodily cues that autistic people use to communicate to one another are hard to describe, much like the way it might be hard for a nonautistic person to explain exactly what cues in another person lead them, for example, to believe that person is snobby. Amanda describes it as something that comes naturally to her the way nonautistic nonverbal communication seems to come easily to nonautistic people.

How Nonautistic Peers Can Help

Michael Crouch—who is in his early thirties, was diagnosed with Pervasive Development Disorder–Not Otherwise Specified (PDD-NOS) at age eleven, and is the college postmaster at the Crown College of the Bible in Tennessee—credits girls with helping him develop good communication skills. Some of his areas of difficulty were public speak-

FOOD FOR THOUGHT

THE IMPACT OF COMMUNICATION ON BEHAVIOR
AS EXPERIENCED BY A NONVERBAL PERSON

As mentioned above, Sue Rubin is a nonverbal autistic young woman, a student at Whittier College, and a disability advocate. The following is an excerpt from Sue's presentation at the Autism Society of America's national conference in 2007.[7] For more information about Sue, visit her website at www.sue-rubin.org.

. . . When I began to type my behaviors were still pretty bad. When I started Whittier high school I was only included for three classes because I was such a mess. Whenever I got scared I very sadly banged my head and attacked my special ed teachers who were supporting me in regular classes. I had to be removed from class numerous times. As I got more comfortable with high school I was able to add more classes. And as I got better at controlling myself I was able to type about what was causing the behavior. Sometimes it was something specific that could be fixed and sometimes it was just being overwhelmed emotionally. Typing allowed me to become an advocate for myself. I really needed competent facilitators and aides who understood how important it was for me to get to class on time and have good notes so I could study for tests.

Typing also allowed me to meet regularly with the educational psychologist so I could tell her what was bothering me. The psychologist was aware of my awful behavior in the past and was anxious to help me. Actually she now lives across the street from me and still is there as a friend to help me.

While I was in high school typing allowed me to write my own social stories and participate in my own behavior plans. Even after I graduated and started college and moved into my own home, I still had behaviors and needed to tell my support staff how they could help me. . . . As I spend more and more time engaged in academics and typing almost whole days I find myself better able to control my behavior. I really believe that my brain has been rewired and the autistic part that was responsible for all that awful behavior is now subservient to the awesome intellectual part that enables me to stop a behavior when I feel it coming. I am also not such an emotional mess. I am able to cope with changes and new situations much better.

Typing allows me to be a college student. Without typing I couldn't have graduated from high school with honors or taken the SAT test. When I am in class now, I *am relaxed and quite comfortable participating in class discussions and relating to other students. My professors all enjoy having me in class and want me to take their other classes.*

Typing also enables me to have real friends, which also helps my behavior. I am happy when I am out with friends and behaviors just don't happen. This has been a long process and I couldn't have done it without extraordinary people in my life— my teachers, school psychologist, speech therapist, and my parents who loved me even when I was impossible to love. I know my story is unusual and is shared only by a handful of people in this country, but that is not because I am unusual. It is because other people with severe behavior problems have not been given a method of communication and the support needed to make the most of it.

ing, speaking too fast or too low, eye contact, and stuttering. When he was a teenager, there were five girls at his church who, every week for two years, encouraged him to sing in the teen choir. He felt he had a bad voice and was scared to get up in front of an audience and sing. Because of their persistence, however, he joined the choir. When he attended college, some of the same girls were his classmates. They once again encouraged him to be a part of the college choir. He says these experiences, plus everyday exercises he learned in a speech class at the college, helped him develop the strong speaking voice he has today.

Conclusion

Challenges with communication can range from a person who is nonverbal to a person who is verbal but understands only the literal meaning of words and phrases. It is important to start as early as possible to instill the idea and purpose of meaningful communication. Consulting with a speech therapist experienced in autism spectrum disorders is useful. Find a system of communication that will work with the child if he cannot use speech in a functional manner. There are many different systems of communications and different ways of teaching them including (but not limited to) the Picture Exchange Communication System (PECS), sign language, learning to point to letters or type using the Rapid Prompting Method (RPM) or facilitated communication (FC), as well as assistive technology. For children who are using speech but having difficulties with understanding the "hidden curriculum" or metaphors or "reading between the lines," there are resources available to teach these young-sters. Whatever the individual needs and challenges are, there are methods and approaches that can help.

3

Safety

I was screaming inside but no one could hear me.
—Jeremy Sicile-Kira, August 2006

We have always had concerns for our son Jeremy's safety, though the particular dangers we've been concerned about have changed over the years. When he was about nine months old, he cut himself on the forehead, requiring a visit to the emergency room for stitches. He was sitting in the living room, reached for a toy, and lost his balance. He did not have the automatic reflex that most babies do to stick out his arm to stop his fall, and he fell onto a plastic, supposedly safe, baby toy that cut into his skin. He never uttered a sound. I found him lying on the floor with blood on his face.

When Jeremy was in elementary school, he could not or would not stop and wait at street corners. Although from his training with the Afternoon Angels (my very apt name for his after-school tutors) and with me, he knew he was supposed to stop at the curb, wait for the change signal, and look for cars right and left before safely crossing the street, his urge to run out to the beautiful bright line in the middle of the road was too strong. He kept trying to get to the yellow line and walk along it. It took many years for him to learn that he had to stop. It was hard to find anything more enticing than the yellow line. Recently Jeremy got an assistant dog that he had been wanting for years, and although the dog is not responsible for keeping Jeremy at the curb, he is a very good prompt. The dog has been taught to do an "automatic sit" when he comes to a curb. This is a good reminder to Jeremy to stop, and the dog is actually more reinforcing than the yellow line.

When Jeremy was in junior high, he came home from school one day with bright red scrape marks on his chest and on his back but with no note or phone call or any sort of explanation from the school. I took him to his doctor, and she identified them as rug burns. The next day I asked the school staff where these marks had come from, and it was reported to me that it probably happened when the inexperienced school district occupational therapist attempted to do some form of sensory integration by dragging my son around the classroom by his arms or legs.

These are just a few of the many examples of safety concerns I have in regard to Jeremy that are linked to his autism. It is a well-known fact that developmentally disabled and nonverbal people—whether they are children, teens, adults, or seniors—are at high risk of being physically and sexually abused—a parent's worst nightmare. I used to think that parents who were on the lookout for possible abusers and feared for their child's safety were paranoid. Not anymore.

Safety Concerns

When a child is young, we focus on basic safety skills such as not touching a hot stove or not playing with sharp scissors and looking both ways before crossing the street. There are additional essential safety skills that need to be focused on as they get older. Personal safety from bullying at school; safety from emotional, physical, or sexual abuse (from individuals known to the child or from strangers); safety from the unwanted attention of another person; safety from unhealthy relationships—these are all areas we as parents need to consider when teaching the concept of safety.

Most adults on the autism spectrum had safety concerns as children, and some continue to do so as adults because of sensory processing challenges, as discussed in Chapter 1. These challenges can make it difficult for children on the spectrum to feel or perceive danger. However, now that there is increased awareness about sensory issues, there are many more therapies and strategies available that can help.

Feeling and being safe and secure are important to everyone's survival. Yet a great majority of adults on the spectrum have personal stories of being bullied or sexually or physically abused as children, teens, or adults. The most alarming part is that some did not even realize at the time that they were being victimized.

Nonverbal children are at a high risk of physical and sexual abuse because of their perceived inability to communicate and also because they tend to be grouped in classrooms or homes or summer camps, where predators know they can find victims. Those on the more able end of the spectrum are at risk because they are not good at reading body language and figuring out a person's intent. Many verbal adults report, with hindsight, that they put themselves in situations that made them easier targets to be victimized. In all situations, empowering children with knowledge is crucial to their safety. It is important to start teaching early some notions of safety as well as how to recognize unsafe situations.

Although we want our children to be safe and to feel safe, as parents and teachers we need to strike a balance between creating a safe environment and letting them experience opportunities that could expand their world and enrich their lives.

Safety and Sensory Processing Challenges

Most children can feel the difference between "toasty warm" and "scalding hot." Most learn fairly quickly not to run into the street, not to open the door to strangers, and not to take rides from people they don't know. However, for many children on the spectrum, these childhood safety issues are not apparent or not easily learned. Safety is one of the main reasons for ensuring that children on the spectrum receive treatment for and learn strategies to help with their sensory processing challenges.

Children on the spectrum are at greater risk of accidentally hurting themselves. In Chapter 1, we discussed sensory processing challenges and how they can affect children differently. Because of their sensory processing difficulties, many have a harder time feeling sensations such as hot and cold, or the sharpness of an object.

Unless a person "feels" the heat of a flame or the sharpness of a knife, he will not understand that fire or knives can be dangerous. Donna Williams, for example, could not feel the difference between nice warm water and hot water that could burn her skin. Occupational therapy with a good therapist who is experienced in sensory integration can be helpful in teaching a parent and school staff techniques for helping a child "feel" sensations better.

Those with visual processing challenges may not see dangers that they may be facing, such as the distance from a tree branch to the ground they want to jump off of, or a moving car in the street. As with the other essential skills, they do not learn about what is safe and not safe by osmosis. These skills have to be taught. The length of time it takes to teach them and the methods to use are different and individual. Usually a good behavior plan can be helpful, especially if paired with social stories. Social stories with visuals that are simple, clear, and read often to the child can be helpful in eventually getting the child to accept responsibility for his actions as he gets older. Even if you think your child is not understanding, it is important to keep showing and reading the social story. It may sink in. The social story should be clear and factual, and read in a calm manner at a time when the child is relaxed (i.e., not during an outburst).

Some children have real challenges when it comes to spatial awareness. A parent describes her seven-year-old son who is on the spectrum and likes to ride his bicycle. Although he can physically ride a bicycle without assistance, he still likes to focus his attention on the rotating back wheel, and she worries about his ability to tear himself away from the rotating wheel to be able to keep a lookout for cars. He gets mesmerized by whatever he is focusing on, to the exclusion of everything else.

PRACTICAL TIP

Because of the immediate dangers of not understanding the necessity of safety rules, it is important to be very clear and firm about situations where a child may get hurt, such as touching a hot stove or running into traffic. In our house, a very strong *no* was reserved for situations that could lead Jeremy to get hurt when he was little—twirling a glass on a hard surface, trying to climb up to places where he shouldn't be. Loud noises were uncomfortable for him, and he learned to stop whatever he was doing when I yelled, "No!" and to wait for further instruction. Then, I would explain clearly and simply that what he was doing was not safe. It is important to find a system for getting your child to stop immediately when he is doing something dangerous.

The Importance of Learning to Ask for Help

In her book, *Life and Love: Positive Strategies for Autistic Adults*, Zosia Zaks explains that turning to trusted nonautistic "helpers" is a vital skill that needs to be learned. Young children on the spectrum do not seek out others for help when they are hurt on the school playground, or their shoe comes untied, and so on, yet this is a skill they should be taught from early on. Learning to ask for help, and later, advice from trusted people will prepare them for different types of social relationships when they are teenagers and then on into adulthood.

Dena Gassner, MSW, is an autism consultant and an advisory board member for both the national organizations of the Autism Society of America and GRASP. She was diagnosed as an adult and is the parent of a teen on the spectrum. Dena suggests that, for small children with Asperger's, shopping in stores can also be a lesson in safety and learning to ask for help. Staying at your small child's side and telling her, "Never be afraid. I will never leave you. You will not get lost," gives the child a sense of security. As the child gets a little bit older, she can be taught the skill of recognizing and approaching someone who works in the store to ask for help, which might be necessary if she gets separated from her parent.

Dena believes that teaching the same safety rules that you would to any child is crucial, such as, "Don't open the door for anyone when you are home alone." What differs, depending on the child's ability level, is how and for how long you teach her. Social stories and practicing the skill (i.e., having known and unknown people come to the door for training purposes) are good ways to reinforce the lesson.

Bullying and Abuse: The Possibility of Becoming a Victim

Bullying

Everyone on the more functionally able end of the spectrum has stories of bullying during their school years. As Luke Jackson describes in the book he wrote as a teenager, *Freaks, Geeks & Asperger Syndrome*, bullying can be physical or verbal, but it is never any fun. His first memory of bullying is from his nursery school days, where he was laughed at often, and that was when he started to feel like he did not fit in. In his first year of elementary school, a group of boys took to pushing and shoving him, and the same set of boys continued this for years until he changed schools. Jerry Newport, author of *Your Life Is Not a Label*, talks about how bullying was rampant in middle school. He advises older autistic students to learn the difference between ordinary teasing and bullying, which is not always apparent to those on the spectrum.

Author Nick Dubin, in his book *Asperger Syndrome and Bullying*, describes not only strategies and solutions but how he was tormented by bullies from an early age. Nick details reasons why people with Asperger's syndrome, particularly children, are easy targets for being bullied. Some of these are gullibility, odd use of language, a low frustration tolerance, auditory processing problems, as well as difficulties in reading nonverbal cues.

Stephen Shore reports that he was subject to a fair amount of bullying as he was growing up. Back then, bullying was considered a phase that everyone went through, a sort of rite of passage.

Although the situation may have gotten somewhat easier now for

> **PRACTICAL TIP**
>
> Principals can put policies into effect and make sure school personnel and students know that bulling is not acceptable. Specific examples of what constitutes bullying should be given. Consequences for any transgression should be made clear. Parents can help their children on the spectrum by teaching them about the "hidden curriculum" (mentioned in Chapter 2) so that they understand expressions and social situations better. Teaching social skills to students on the spectrum will also help them be less at risk.

students on the spectrum, I still meet parents and professionals in my travels around the country who are seeking advice and resources to combat bullying. Many of them report not getting much support from school administration because of a lack of awareness about Asperger's syndrome. Neurotypical adults do not always understand the social and communication deficits of a child or teen on the more functionally able end of the spectrum. If a child is doing well academically, they don't understand why he doesn't just "get" the social stuff. Principals are the ones who set the tone at schools, and they should become aware of the difficulties and ensure that bullying will not be tolerated. Bullying is a school problem, not an individual or personal problem, and should be treated as such.

Sometimes, instead of the tormentor, it is the child on the spectrum who gets reprimanded. This happens all too often. Temple Grandin recalls that, as a teenager, she was teased and called "tape recorder" by the other students (of course, out of earshot of school staff). When she finally could not tolerate it any longer, she threw a book at one of the students. Temple was the one who got kicked out of school. Although we hope to lessen and eliminate bullying, we also need to teach our children how to respond appropriately to bullying situations so that they are not punished twice.

For the more able child, teen, and adult who may have good communication skills and are integrated most of the time, they risk being victimized. Unless they have been taught, they do not know by osmosis or learn from their friends (they usually have few) what constitutes a sexual act, how to withhold consent, and so on. This happens also because they are poor at predicting behaviors, because they are gullible by nature, and because they don't understand the "hidden curriculum." The inability to pick up on social cues and body language—unless they've been taught—puts individuals on the spectrum in a more vulnerable position and makes them an easy target for bullies and sexual predators.

Dena Gassner believes that all children need to be taught how to be assertive early on. She explains that being able to protect yourself from an invasion of your privacy is an essential safety skill that begins with assertiveness. For example, teaching a young child to independently order food in a restaurant and to clarify what she wants (with or without assistive technology for those who are nonverbal) is one way of teaching about appropriate assertiveness. Learning to be specific in requesting what she wants or doesn't want when little is a great way of planting the first seeds of advocating for oneself. For example, this same child as a teenager will have the confidence and experience to say no when pressured by peers to cut classes to participate in activities that are not good choices such as doing drugs or drinking and driving. Also, she will find it easier to say no if someone who is irresponsible asks to "borrow" an expensive or prized possession.

Bullying and Emotional Abuse from Unthinking Adults

Sometimes, emotional abuse can come from adults who are there to help the child. Often, the adult is not even aware of the detrimental effect of what they are saying and doing. Examples of this include the teacher who tells a young male student to "suck it up and act like a man" or the general education teacher who berates a teenager for missing homework assignments because the student can't copy down the assignment written on the chalkboard while listening to the lesson being taught (multitasking difficulties).

Nick Dubin remembers how some teachers reinforced his own feelings of shame, resulting in low self-esteem. For example, when he was in high school, Nick had a very uneven motor skill profile. He was the best singles player on the varsity tennis team, which required good gross motor skills, yet he could not tie his own shoes due to poor fine motor skills. The teachers thought Nick wasn't trying hard enough and criticized him when he was, in fact, trying very hard. This, in turn, lowered his self-esteem.

Author and advocate Michael John Carley recalls how teachers at the school he attended made jokes directed at him during class, which encouraged peer disrespect and led to bullying of a verbal nature outside the classroom.

Emotional abuse occurs in special education classes as well. Professionals take the liberty of carrying on a discussion about a nonverbal child in front of him as if the child were deaf and could not hear. For example, an occupational therapist once began a discussion with the classroom teacher in my son's presence about the doubtful benefit of mainstreaming Jeremy in a general education classroom. She stated that Jeremy was "workshop material" and would be spending his adult life in sheltered workshops, so it was a waste of time to put him in mainstream environments, and that it was unrealistic for his parents to think that he might benefit from them. This therapist did not realize that Jeremy understood what she was saying—and that the incident had a detrimental effect on his behavior and self-esteem.

Inappropriate Relationships with Adults

Sometimes, adults working with developmentally delayed children have behaviors toward a child that may be considered appropriate at a certain age, but are not appropriate as the child gets older. For example, when Beth went to pick up her twelve-year-old son from summer day camp one year, he was sitting in his camp counselor's lap and she was hugging him and rumpling his hair, and talking about how much she loved him. This kind of behavior is totally inappropriate and very confusing to a preteen boy in the throes of puberty, whether or not he is on the spectrum. Of course we want our children to be loved, but no matter how young or

FOOD FOR THOUGHT

THE POSSIBILITY OF ABUSE

Joshua D. Feder, MD, is a child and family psychiatrist in Solana Beach, California, with a practice focused on helping persons with autism and other developmental disorders, teaching, and research. He has served on the US Navy Headquarters Team for Investigation of Child Sexual Abuse and as reviewer for the journal *Child Maltreatment*, and he currently sits on the Ethics Committee of the San Diego Psychiatric Society, a chapter of the American Psychiatric Association. Dr. Feder has this advice for parents:

We typically start wondering whether something has happened only after there is a change in a child's behavior. Then, we look at all the things that might account for the change, for example, "Is she sick?" "The staff isn't doing the right things with him." "He's scared of the water." "The meds are wrong." People wonder about physical or sexual abuse only as an afterthought. But it's best to be proactive. Do background checks on the people working with your child. Ensure that there are policies in place that make it mandatory to never leave a child with only one adult.

I have my own "clinical" biases when it comes to individuals working with kids. I like to know that the person working with the child has healthy relationships with appropriate other people, e.g., an adult guy has a good and functioning marriage, or a teenage kid has a significant other of the same age and a decent set of friendships too. You want to know that the person working with your child or family member has an active and healthy way of getting his or her relationship needs met, so he or she is at less risk of falling into an inappropriate relationship with your child/family member.

I get a bad feeling when I learn of a person who is so devoted to the kids and does not have healthy outside relationships. That's another good guideline: if you are getting a weird feeling about something, trust your gut and talk to a trusted person about it. Most often if you have a competent and experienced mental health professional, that professional can help you think through what's going on with a clear-headed approach. Pay attention to "boundary crossings" on the part of staff such as changes in usual rules like stretching the time of camp or appointments, after-hours extra time, or anything that marks the relationship as different or "special." While close relationships can develop between staff and families, those relationships lose their objectivity and their helpfulness when the professional (teacher, staff member, therapist, etc.) starts getting their own needs met through the relationship with the child/family member/client family. This can be subtle, such as in expecting cookies from a parent, to more obvious "boundary violations" such as doing business together separate from the initial helping relationship. Subtle slides can lead to serious breaches, including sexual abuse of our very vulnerable kids and family members.

It sounds crass, but the main reason that people should be working with your kids/family members is that is it their job, how they make their living. Of course you hope the person loves their job, likes your kid, etc., but when a staff member loses sight of the main objective—the job—that's when things start to become unclear and unhelpful. Does that mean you need to be suspicious of anything altruistic, volunteer, or other work "beyond the call of duty"? Well, yes and no. Be grateful but also be careful. Guys generally are not interested in other people's children, and guys—infused as they are with testosterone—are usually more naturally predatory in their sexual behavior. That can work fine in healthy courting, but it is a problem when the person does not have the skills to relate in appropriate relationships and then instead gravitates toward other, less appropriate targets of sexual desire. There are plenty of instances of females who sexually abuse others, but the typical story involves males abusing male and/or female victims.

Children who have been abused can demonstrate such a wide variety of symptoms that it is difficult to distinguish from other conditions. Depression, anxiety, over-activity, aggression, perseveration, toilet regression, dysregulation and other symptoms are not specific but are often the main kinds of responses to abuse. Specific symptoms may crop up, such as playing out sexual acts, talking about sexual things especially out of developmental context. When a child claims to have been abused, the best thing to do is to have a competent professional evaluate what is going on. Remember that it is a bad idea to keep repeating the story with the child, as this muddies the child's memory (whether verbal or not).

A person who is showing behavioral changes, for whatever reason, deserves attention, protection, and treatment. Treatment for sexual abuse depends on how the person has been affected, the individual characteristics of the person abused, and family circumstances. That is a topic for another time.

A version of this article first appeared in *Valerie's List*, an informative e-newsletter for the autism community published at www.valerieslist.com by Valerie Saraf.

how old they are, signs of endearment should be shown in an appropriate manner befitting the relationship.

The Need to Inform from an Early Age

Sometimes, bullying can be of a sexual nature. Although parents of young children may feel they do not have to be concerned about such problems, the seeds for preventing this kind of bullying can be sown at an early age. Dena Gassner believes that although it is hard for parents to think of their child as a future adult with a healthy sex life, they should be concerned about ensuring that their children learn the safety skills of assertiveness and advocacy, as mentioned earlier, so they can protect themselves from being sexually bullied or abused. Dena says that assertiveness and advocacy are the cornerstone to being able to develop a healthy sexual identity as an adult.

As children get older, they need to be learning about puberty and about sex and sexual activity. Although they may not be emotionally maturing at the same rate as their peers, they need to understand what their nonautistic peers are talking about so they don't get into trouble. For example, a parent shared the story of what happened to her daughter Anne, who has Asperger's syndrome. Anne was fully included in high school, and she really wanted to be friends with a particular group of popular girls. These teen girls did not know Anne had Asperger's as her diagnosis had not been disclosed, but they could tell she was not like them. They just thought she was weird. They picked up on the fact that she wanted to be their friend, so they told her she could be their friend if Anne went to Philip and did a certain thing with him and came back and told them when she had done it. So Anne went to Philip and performed oral sex on him—not realizing that this was a sex act—and promptly went back to the girls to tell them.

The same rules apply in elementary school as in junior high or high school: the need for community awareness, knowing what constitutes appropriate behavior, self-esteem, assertiveness training, and how to advocate for yourself. In the true personal story related above, the situation could have been prevented by a combination of factors. First of all,

PRACTICAL TIP

When young, children should be taught about their bodies, learning to name the different parts. They should also be taught about what areas of their body no one else should touch, as well as to communicate to a trusted adult if someone has done so. As they get a bit older, teaching them matter-of-factly about the birds and the bees is a good idea. As they enter the teen years, they need to be taught about their changing bodies, more about sexuality, what constitutes a sex act, along with your ethical and moral beliefs as a parent about age-appropriate and inappropriate behavior. This will help your child stay out of dicey and unsafe situations.

the neurotypical students on campus should be made aware of the autism spectrum and what that means in terms of positive aspects for the student on the spectrum, but also the difficulties the student may experience. (MTV's *True Life*: "I Have Autism" did a good job of explaining to teenagers what autism looks like without making it seem like a negative). Second, it should be made clear that there is zero tolerance for bullying among students. Period. Third, the student with Asperger's should be taught a certain amount of self-esteem and assertiveness training. And most important, Anne should have been taught about what constitutes a sexual act and under what circumstance a person chooses as an adult to have or not to have sex.

Many times parents and teachers are reluctant about teaching preteens or teenagers on the spectrum about sex. They assume that they are not ready or not interested in sex or dating, not realizing that it is this lack of knowledge that makes them potential victims. Sometimes a student will sit through general education health classes and it is assumed that the student has understood how the information relates to him personally. But although children with Asperger's on the more able end of the spectrum can usually learn and memorize information, they often have difficulties generalizing information or realizing how the information relates to them personally.

Teaching at an Early Age Prepares Children for Adult life

When I was discussing social relationships with Zosia Zaks, she shared that safety supports for the social aspect of life are crucial for people on the spectrum. Having a trusted nonautistic person to bounce things off of is necessary because of the autistic individual's trusting nature and way of thinking, which puts her at a greater risk for sexual abuse or violence. Again, possible clues from tone of voice or posture on the part of a predator go unnoticed. Also knowing when to apply rules such as "Don't go home with a stranger" is difficult because, if you just met the person and have exchanged pleasantries, or have "met" over the Internet, he or she is no longer a stranger in the literal sense of the word to someone on the spectrum.

For example, a social worker relates the story of her Asperger's daughter, Jill, wanting to move into her own place at the age of twenty-two, which she did. She had a job and was competent as far as her functional and daily living skills, had been explained about sex, but had no practical experience with dating. Jill did not have personal experiences to draw from about the different types of relationships, including the responsibilities or safety factors inherent to getting to know and having an intimate relationship with another adult. She also did not possess "common sense." Soon after moving into her own apartment, Jill decided she wanted to experience sex, and joined an online singles dating service. She met someone online and made a "date" with a male to meet her at her apartment, where he violently forced himself on her, then stole whatever he could from the apartment. The police were not very helpful. There was physical evidence, but the authorities did not have an understanding of Asperger's syndrome and how Jill could not have anticipated that inviting a stranger into her apartment was not a safe thing to do.

Zosia suggests that adults on the spectrum make a Safe Activities List (such as meeting someone in the daytime at a coffee shop, where there will be other people; walking home from campus by yourself during daylight hours along busy streets, where you will not be all alone; etc.). The idea of a Safe Activities List can be adapted for young children. Starting a list when they are young, going over it often, and incorporating different appropriate safe activities as time goes on will help the child think about safety first rather than act impulsively.

In her book *Pretending to Be Normal: Living with Asperger's Syndrome*, Liane Holliday Willey shares a personal example of how the combination of her sensory processing challenges and her trusting nature put her in an unsafe situation. As a college professor, she was in the habit of getting to campus very early in the morning to avoid the many sensory overloads that could be caused by traffic, noise, and sticky weather. One morning, soon after she had arrived in her empty classroom, a male visitor she did not recognize entered the room. Liane remembers being more annoyed by the look of him (old worn clothes) than by the fact that he was there very early in the morning and approaching her, telling her he had just been released from jail. She relates being more engrossed by his moldy appearance than alarmed that he was approaching her. As he violated her personal space, she became disturbed, but it was mainly because of his offensive smell. She recounts that she did not think of screaming or running away as he came closer; she was unable to separate her emotions from her sensory overload. Luckily for her, one of her male students arrived and quickly walked over to them and put himself between Liane and the other man, who left in a flash.

Private and Public Behaviors Need to Be Taught at an Early Age

Teaching the child appropriate behaviors in various circumstances is really the best prevention. For example, one evening while attending a family pool party organized by a local autism organization, I was approached by a man who had brought his teenage daughter for a swim. He asked if I wouldn't mind going into the women's changing area while his daughter was in there just to make sure she was safe. I felt a bit uncomfortable with this request as I did not know the girl or her family, but he told me she was completely independent in her dressing skills, and it was just to make sure nothing happened to her. We went into the women's changing area, but I stayed as far away as possible from her to give her privacy. I stood near the door so I could see if people were entering the room, and I had my back turned to her. However, as she was getting

---

PRACTICAL TIP

Teach the notions of "private" and "public" by having two picture icons: one that says "public" showing a stick figure that is clothed, and one that says "private" showing a stick figure wearing only underwear. Then, place the private icon inside the bathroom and bedroom door, and the public icon outside the bedroom/bathroom door (this can be done in classrooms where appropriate). The child is then taught that he can get undressed in his room or bathroom (some may need a behavior plan for this as well) but not in the public areas of the house. When the child takes his clothes off outside the private areas, he is told, "No, this is a public area. It is not appropriate to take your clothes off," and shown the icon. Then, he is taken to his room or bathroom and shown the private icon, and told, "This is the private area. You are allowed to take your clothes off here." If and when the child begins to show masturbation behaviors, he should be directed to his room using the same notion of behavior to be done in private only.

---

changed, she kept coming closer to me and talking and asking if I wanted to be her friend, repeating it very often as if she was stimming on a social phrase she had learned as appropriate. Unfortunately, it was not appropriate given the fact that she was in various states of undress and I was a complete stranger, at least from a neurotypical viewpoint.

I kept thinking, "Someone has got to teach this teen appropriate behavior for these kinds of situations and in dressing rooms, or she will find herself in serious trouble one day and not even know it." I was also wondering: "Does she do this when she is changing for PE class? Is the school addressing it? Do the parents know? Are the parents trying to teach her about appropriate public and private behavior?"

Teaching the concepts of "private" and "public" to children from an early age (no matter what the ability level) will be extremely useful to them as they get older because it will facilitate teaching about things you do in private (e.g., get dressed, use the toilet, get undressed, touch certain parts of your body). As they get older, the notion of private and public will be helpful for explaining the appropriateness of conversation (whether verbal or typing or using other forms of communication) in different types of social relationships (see Chapter 8). They will be able to understand the concept of private conversations (with Mom and Dad and your best friend) and appropriate public conversations (at the cafeteria table with classmates).

Physical and Sexual Abuse

Even harder to discuss are physical and sexual abuse. To be honest, many parents would rather not know about the risks, yet when it happens to their child, they wonder how it is they could have been so ignorant about the dangers of abuse.

The concerns around the issue of abuse are of equal importance no matter where a child, teen, or adult is on the spectrum. It may just be of a different kind. A nonverbal child who needs a one-on-one aide; an adult who requires twenty-four-hour support staff; and children and adults who have little or no communication skills and are in self-contained classrooms, special camps, and segregated living and working facilities are at high risk because predators looking for victims know this is where they are grouped and also because they know there is very little likelihood of their being caught as the victims either will not be able to communicate or they will not be believed.

The parents of a preteen girl, Michelle, shared with me the story of how they caught a neighborhood boy she had grown up with (a trusted person) performing a sexual act with her. Apparently, this had been going on for some time. Although there was physical evidence, the authorities were unable to do anything to ensure their daughter's safety from the young male. They had a very difficult time keeping this person away from their daughter 24/7 as he lived next door and his parents refused to accept any responsibility for the situation. This abusive situation created stress for the whole family. Michelle no longer trusts males, which has affected the relationship she has with her brother and her father. Getting appropriate therapy for Michelle, as well as the family, who all suffered

FOOD FOR THOUGHT

MORE ON THE POSSIBILITY OF ABUSE

Dr. Nora Baladerian, PhD, a licensed psychologist in California, is the director of the Disability, Abuse and Personal Rights Project. She has been working with families and individuals with disabilities in the areas of crime victimization including sexual assault since 1972, and is the recipient of the 2008 National Crime Victims Service Award. She has this advice to offer:

Children with disabilities have many of the same needs as any other child, for education, family, safety, recreation, among many others. Most parents of children with disabilities receive information and guidance on these aspects of life, but nearly none on the problems of child abuse, sexual assault, molestation, or other types of maltreatment that they may experience. Knowledge is power, and when parents and other family members are aware that their child (or adult family member) who has a significant disability is more likely to be targeted for abuse than other children, they are more likely to implement the risk reduction strategies available to them. Although data on abuse of adults with disabilities is scarce, research on children with disabilities finds that they become victims of abuse at 3.4 times the rate of children who do not have disabilities (Sullivan, T., and Knutson, D., 2001). While many agree that abuse occurs more, those who specialize in the field of abuse and disability believe that for both children and adults, increased victimization is more likely 10 times the rate than for those without disabilities.

Who are the perpetrators? Research shows that they are persons who have found their way into the lives of children with disabilities as trusted care and service providers. They may be program directors or volunteers at recreational programs; 1–1 aides (paraprofessionals) on school campus or teachers; bus drivers or psychologists; medical doctors; speech therapists; rehabilitation, vocational, or other specialists. Perpetrators are individuals in the home, on the bus, in the day program (school or work), or support services. These are people who have gained the trust of the child/adult with a disability and their family members.

Often it comes as a shock both to the victim of abuse and to the family members when abuse occurs and is disclosed. Most often, the abuse is never reported. Many times victims never tell their family members, or they may tell them months or years after it happened. Some show signs right away, such as sudden changes in mood, sleeping or eating patterns, a refusal to go to a particular place or with a

particular person. It is essential for the parents to act immediately upon their suspicions of abuse and see their doctor or report their suspicions to the appropriate
agency (Department of Child and Family Services, Adult Protective Services, or the
local police or sheriff's office.)

The signs of abuse are about the same for children with and without disabilities,
verbal and nonverbal. These include primarily a change from the norm. Signs can
be emotional such as crying or sadness, anger, irritability, sassiness, rage, self-
hurting, becoming very aggressive or very withdrawn, not wanting to return to
camp or the day program, or other location such as a park or the beach. Other
related problems may be the onset of nightmares, wanting to sleep with one's parents, changes in eating, toileting, and clothing preferences and behavior. There
can be questions to the parents that had never been asked before about sexuality
issues such as pregnancy. Also, there may a regression to a younger level of
achievement or maturity, such as needing help with toileting, dressing, or getting
ready for the next activity. Do not take the children back to a location they have
said they don't want to go, before you check it out. As a parent, you will want support and consultation as well. Dangers of sexual and other types of abuse exist
about equally for boys and girls. Do not think that if your child is a boy, he is
immune from abuse.

As with any other danger in the community, it is important for children to know
that maltreatment exists, and what to do if it occurs, just as you do with crossing
the street with the green light, and other safety matters. They should know that
maltreatment may come in the form of physical, sexual, verbal, or emotional
abuse, or neglect such as not being provided with educational services along with
other children (being put in "time out" all day), not being given their medication,
or being left out of certain school activities. In these cases, the child should make
this known to the parent, who can take corrective action. Of course, the child may
feel sad or angry or even guilty or ashamed of what has been done to him. In addition, the parent may feel guilty for not protecting his child sufficiently. However, it
must be said that no matter how prepared or careful anyone is, abuse can still happen. It is essential to be aware of this, and to be psychologically equipped to
respond calmly and effectively.

Parents can acquire more information about how to protect their children and
to respond when abuse is suspected or disclosed by visiting the website www
.disability-abuse.com. This site provides a great deal of information as well as
serving as a portal to other sites with further information. When we wish to close
our eyes and minds to a terrible and terrifying fact of life, we just leave our loved

ones vulnerable and alone. It is essential to be informed and implement the risk reduction strategies available to every family and agency. You may want to look in particular for the "Risk Reduction Guidebook for Parents and Advocates of Children and Adults with Developmental Disabilities," available through this site.

A version of this article first appeared in *Valerie's List*, an informative e-newsletter for the autism community published at www.valerieslist.com by Valerie Saraf.

◼ ◼ ◼ ◼ ◼ ◼ ◼ ◼ ◼ ◼

from post-traumatic stress disorder (PTSD), was impossible in the town they lived in, so they had to travel a far distance to get the therapy that was needed.

Michael, a nonverbal teenager, attended a summer day camp for autistic teens, which he had attended for two previous years and had thoroughly enjoyed. After two days of camp, he refused to go back, stopped sleeping at night, refused to go swimming (his favorite activity), and exhibited behaviors unlike him, but typical of abuse victims. A week later, Michael requested to see a doctor and informed his doctor, his mother, his tutor, and a trauma therapist by typing about how he was victimized at camp.

Unfortunately, situations such as these can and do happen. For some advice on this difficult topic, see the two "Food for Thought" sections in this chapter, both written by two experts.

Conclusion

Children on the spectrum are more at risk for hurting themselves because of their sensory processing challenges. For those who have trouble feeling extreme temperatures or sharpness or falls, there are many sensory integration techniques that may help their bodies "feel." For those with no notion of safety, social stories can be helpful for explaining *why* we need to be careful, and behavior modification techniques can help teach the behaviors that can help keep them safe. As they get older, the children who appear less impacted by autism become more at risk for bullying, either because they cannot read the social cues of the others their age and become victims, or because they may appear annoying to those who do not know about autism. Children as they get older need to be taught more and more about the "hidden curriculum," social skills, relationships, and dating so they can have a better understanding of their peers. All children need to be taught about appropriate and inappropriate behavior toward others and toward themselves so that they do not inadvertently victimize someone else and get in trouble, or become victims themselves. They need to be taught clear rules of expected behavior or what to do in certain situations, such as asking for help.

There also needs to be more teaching about autism awareness to nonautistic peers, school administrators, the public, police, justice and criminal systems, in order to reduce bullying as well as minimize the risk of sexual and physical abuse. Care should be taken to inform the child without making him anxious—how you say it is just as important as what you say. We want to teach our children to be safe but still allow them to experience opportunities that will enrich their lives and help them grow into adulthood.

4

Self-Esteem

I AM POEM

I am a brother to a cool girl
I wonder about the future
I hear music with guitars playing
I like music, and books about other people,
guitar music, Spanish and reggae
I see beautiful colors
I am not a label
I pretend I can talk
I feel lucky that I have people that believe in me
I am like you and I feel, too, like you do inside
I touch a lot of things to know more
I worry no one will take care of me when I am older
I cry when I am hurt
I am a French American
I understand French and English
I say good people are the ones who respect others
I dream about a better world

I try to behave and not to have too many weird behaviors
I hope to have my own business
Pay more attention to me and less to the label of autism
I am unique

—Jeremy Sicile-Kira,
English Class, February 2006

Jeremy is a complicated young man who people cannot judge on appearance. A good metaphor would be to describe Jeremy as an artichoke. Each leaf on the artichoke has to be taken separately, each having its own characteristics. As you go through each layer of the leaves, it becomes more apparent that there might be something inside, something worth getting to. It takes time to get there, but there is a heart inside, worth the time and effort to expose, as some people say is the prize for the patience of delving through the layers of leaves. Jeremy is this man.

—Allan Gustafson, spring 2007

Ever since Jeremy and his sister, Rebecca, were children, I have done my best to surround them with positive-thinking people. They know they are loved, they know we accept them for who they are, but we expect them both to try hard to reach their potential. Jeremy is impacted by autism, and Rebecca is nonautistic, yet I have the same expectations for them both.

Although Jeremy could not really express himself until recently, I have always spoken to him and in front of him as if he is listening and understanding and as if he is smart. I have never talked down to him. I have always insisted he be mainstreamed in general education classes for a good part of the day. My feeling was, if worst came to worst and he wasn't able to understand the subject matter, at least he was with nondisabled peers for a good part of the day.

There have been many times that I have had to take a stand against the school system. I have removed Jeremy from schools at different times, and run home programs. I believe that every human being is deserving of respect, and that means believing that a child is capable of learning. If a child is not learning, it is not because a child cannot, but rather that we have fallen short in our methods and that we need to be more creative in our approaches to make a connection and have an impact.

Because I think this way, and because his teachers, instructional aides, and the Afternoon Angels believe in Jeremy, he has good self-esteem. He knows that he is very disabled by his autism, but like the rest of us, he focuses on the positive—he is smart, he can communicate, and he can write.

Jeremy and Rebecca know that whatever their dreams and choices are for the future, we will encourage them and help them learn the skills they need to be the best they can be as productive and caring adults.

Take Equal Parts of Acceptance and Expectation and Mix Well

We think we can; therefore, we can. Children form an image of them-selves based on what they hear about themselves and how people treat them. For all children, on or off the spectrum, confidence in one's abili-ties is a necessary precursor to a happy adult life. Having a teacher who looks beyond the behaviors to the essential core of a child, a teacher who takes the time to uncover, layer by layer, the student, to discover the potential of the person inside, as Allan did with Jeremy, is a major factor in developing self-esteem for someone on the spectrum. Having Allan as a teacher during the crucial high school teenage years was what helped my son mature into the personable self-advocating young man he is today.

From my interviews with adults on the spectrum—those severely impacted by autism as well as those with Asperger's syndrome—it is clear that people on the spectrum who appear self-confident and have good self-esteem tend to have had a few things in common while grow-ing up. Having parents or caretakers who were accepting of their child yet expected them to reach their potential and sought out ways to help them was the most important factor. One or two favorite teachers or mentors could see their potential, supported their interests, and expected them to learn and provided strategies to help them. Also helpful were trusted nonautistic peers and autistic peers as well.

Although good self-esteem is a necessary trait in life, rarely does it get mentioned in any curriculum geared toward children on the spectrum. Self-esteem is important because a child needs to believe in his abilities and his worth to continue trying, and because people respect those who give off an aura of being worthy of respect. For a teen to understand he has rights (including the right to be safe and not be a victim, as well as the right to say no), he must feel he has worth, and this all relates back to self-esteem.

Rising to High Expectations

It is a well-known fact that nonautistic children rise to the expectations we have for them. The same is true of autistic children. Temple Grandin's autism was so severe that her mother was advised to institutionalize her, but her mother refused to accept that future for her daughter. In *Unwritten Rules of Social Relationships*, Temple credits high expectations from her parents and teachers, clearly defined behavior rules and consistently applied consequences, as well as strong internal motivation as major factors for her becoming the person she is today. Temple says her mother fostered a high sense of self-esteem in her because she unconsciously realized two important things: that self-esteem is built little by little through real accomplishments, and that the literal, concrete mind of the autistic child needs self-esteem to be built through tangible achievements, combined with verbal praise. Temple also believes strongly that low expectations are dangerous for those on the autism spectrum, and that we need to continually raise the bar higher and higher.

Soma Mukhopadhyay is one of those great teachers who expects her students to learn, and so they do. It is Soma who first taught Jeremy academics and from whom I learned how to teach my son in a way that kept his interest and that eventually, over time, led to a communication skill. Her son, Tito, is a young adult with autism who has had a few books published. In *The Mind Tree: A Miraculous Child Breaks the Silence of Autism*, Tito describes what it was like growing up severely impacted by autism and unable to control or "order" his muscles to move. Tito's mother developed a method of working with her son, now called the Rapid Prompting Method (see "Food for Thought," page 73). Originally brought over by Portia Iverson of Cure Autism Now (CAN), who wanted to learn more about how Tito's brain worked, Soma is now educational director of Helping Autism Through Learning and Outreach (HALO). Soma has used the Rapid Prompting Method to teach academics to more than 600 people with autism, from children to adults (including Jeremy).

Learning to communicate by typing has also been a long process for Sue Rubin, writer and subject of the award-winning documentary *Autism Is a World*. She has stated in presentations that she could not have done it without extraordinary people in her life—her teachers, school psychologist, speech therapist, and her parents—people who believed in her. Sue was first introduced to facilitated communication when she was in eighth grade by her speech therapist at school. She went on to be mainstreamed in high school and graduated with a high GPA. She is currently a student at Whittier College. Her mom and dad used to do three to four hours of homework with her every night and one full day on the weekend for many years. Eventually, they hired tutors, who then helped Sue focus on her homework.

Another example of a nonverbal autistic boy with good self-esteem is DJ Savarese, whose father, Ralph James Savarese, wrote *Reasonable People: A Memoir of Autism and Adoption*, which recounts the story of his and Emily's adoption of DJ, a nonverbal autistic boy. They insist on DJ being fully included in the schools, and for years they taught him literary skills and eventually he began to type slowly and laboriously. Ralph and Emily chose to adopt DJ knowing he was severely impacted by autism. Emily was experienced with autism and is an inclusion specialist. In November 2007, DJ and his family were highlighted on an *Anderson Cooper 360°* show that also included Amanda Baggs. Soon after the show aired, I asked DJ by email what helped him acquire good self-esteem, and this was his reply: "Fresh ideas about autism assume i am free. the cnn interview treated my real self as good, this got my real self strong. Hurts self-esteem if greatly pitied by others."

As mentioned in Chapter 2, my son, Jeremy, began to excel when his

FOOD FOR THOUGHT

ASSUMING INTELLIGENCE AND THE ABILITY TO LEARN

Soma Mukhopadhyay developed the Rapid Prompting Method (RPM) to teach her own son, Tito, who is a published writer despite his autism. Soma is the educational director of Helping Autism Through Learning and Outreach (HALO), a nonprofit organization that provides RPM instruction in its Austin, Texas, clinic. RPM is instruction for improving academic success leading toward communication for persons with autism and similar challenges. The following information is from the HALO website, www.halo-soma.org:

Building the students' self-esteem is an important aspect of RPM. Because of the lack of social initiation and communication skills inherent to those severely affected by their autism, parents and educators sometimes get into the habit of "talking down" to nonverbal students, as opposed to communicating with intelligence, substance and sophistication in language. This notion should not be mistaken to mean that ASD students learn and understand just like everyone else. They do need instruction individualized to open learning channels. But when treated with confidence, ASD students (just like typical students) are more hopeful and sure about themselves and their potential. Assumed intelligence and age-appropriate instruction should not be misconstrued as implying that students already know all of their academics. It does imply that students are very able to learn. Also, it emphasizes the importance of exposure to information and access to knowledge. Students must be exposed to interesting and varied topics if they are ever to gain more knowledge.

Teaching and learning is an age-old process. It does not take scientific research to realize that children must be taught if they are ever to learn and improve. ASD students need not be deprived of teaching and learning opportunities because of diagnosis, differences, or doubt about a student's potential.

teacher, Allan, realized that Jeremy's negative behaviors were an indication that he was bored with the lessons Allan was trying to teach him. As soon as Allan presented more difficult academic work, Jeremy started paying attention and the behaviors decreased. There was no miracle here; it has been years of hard work teaching Jeremy to be able to listen and point to letters and to spell. But he would never have been able to do it if he had not been surrounded by people such as Allan who believed in him and expected him to learn. We all need to be surrounded by people who believe in us, but this is especially true for those who have such a hard time with sensory processing and getting their bodies to "work," people who were considered to be retarded at one time or another—people like Jeremy, Tito, Sue, and DJ. They have been able to learn to communicate and be more functionally able because somehow their paths crossed with people who had high expectations, people who were able to put in the enormous time and energy that it takes to help overcome such obstacles.

How We Talk About Children on the Spectrum

The old saying "Sticks and stones may break my bones, but words will never harm me" is simply not true for children who are still trying to make sense of the world and who are unable to stick up for themselves, either because they are nonverbal or because they don't know how to defend themselves in an appropriate manner. Yet these children often hear negative messages, no matter where they are on the spectrum.

As discussed in Chapter 3, "Safety," verbal bullying by other students and unthinking adults—all too common for kids on the spectrum—can damage a child's self-esteem. As parents, it is hard to be perfect 24/7, and we all have been guilty at one time or another (even with our nonautistic children) of carrying on negative conversations in front of them or of losing our temper for one transgression or another. More disturbing is when a professional in a school setting discusses a nonverbal child in negative terms in front of him, as if the child were deaf or incapable of understanding—or berates him in front of the class for his behavior.

As parents and professionals, we have to be careful of how we discuss

PRACTICAL TIP

Often we are not aware of the negative vocabulary we use or how we talk to the people we spend the most time with. To hear what your child may be taking in every day, set a tape recorder or videotape on at home for a few hours every day over a week. Listen to it, and see if there is negative language or pessimistic messages in regard to autism inadvertently being repeated on a consistent basis. Then, think of other ways the family members could express themselves on this topic in a more positive way.

our children and their challenges in their presence, because what we say does affect them. Discussions of their difficulties within their earshot without giving equal time to their positive attributes can, in the long run, be detrimental. So can discussions about "curing" their autism, because if their autism doesn't go away even with all the treatments, they will always think something is wrong with them, that their parents are disappointed. This is not to say that we should not do everything in our power to help our children; it is more about being careful what we say. For example, most people who talk about curing autism are, in fact, trying to cure the medical problems causing autistic-like symptoms—such as immune system deficiencies, sensory processing challenges, and obsessive behaviors. It is far more positive for the child to hear your discussions about building up the immune system or helping with sensory processing challenges, than it is for him to hear about curing autism.

When it comes to semantics, there is huge disagreement in the autism community about the words that are used. Words such as "disability," "disease," and "cure" bring out strong emotions, often pitting the parents of young children against adults with Asperger's syndrome, as demonstrated by the series of articles on the issue of using the word "cure" in relation to autism, initiated by Alison Singer of Autism Speaks and Michael John Carley of GRASP.

FOOD FOR THOUGHT

WE ARE WHAT WE HEAR, SO WATCH WHAT YOU SAY

Dr. Masaru Emoto is a pioneering Japanese researcher known for his study of how thoughts and feelings affect physical reality. Dr. Emoto, a graduate of the Yokohama Municipal University and the Open International University as a doctor of alternative medicine, has been able to show how different focused "intentions" have an effect on water. Various intentions, when communicated through written and spoken words and music, have differing effects on water samples, and the water appears to "change its expression."

Dr. Emoto developed a technique using a very powerful microscope in a very cold room along with high-speed photography, to photograph newly formed crystals of frozen water samples. He discovered that crystals formed in frozen water reveal changes when specific, concentrated thoughts are directed toward them. He found that water from clear springs or that has been exposed to loving words (through written labels on the containers, spoken words, and music) shows brilliant, complex, and colorful snowflake patterns. In contrast, polluted water or water exposed to negative thoughts forms incomplete, asymmetrical patterns with dull colors. His photographs were first featured in his published books, *Messages from Water 1 and 2*.

Dr. Emoto's newest book, *The Hidden Messages in Water*, further explores his revolutionary research. Since humans and the earth are composed mostly of water, the ramifications of his research are widespread. The implications of this research create a new awareness of how "Sticks and stones may break my bones, but words will never harm me" is actually not true, and the words we use may have not only a psychological effect on people, but also a physiological effect. Thus, "Say nothing unless you have something nice to say" may be old-fashioned but good, healthy advice.

In *Asperger's from the Inside Out: A Supportive and Practical Guide for Anyone with Asperger's Syndrome*, Michael John Carley has created a wonderful table listing the characteristics of Asperger's syndrome. The table lists the characteristics, along with the negative interpretation and the positive interpretation. For example, the characteristic "Says whatever comes into their head, unaware of the potential damage the statement might cause" can be interpreted as either "The individual is rude," or "The individual is honest." Or "Problems with nonartistic activities or fields of study" can be interpreted as "Can be seen as goofing off or not focused on serious matters," or "May be indications of a great, creative mind." Taking a positive look at characteristics can help us come up with ways of being supportive to a child's strengths and not always focusing on the deficits.

Deciding Whether to Tell a Child About His Diagnosis

For parents of children who are severely impacted by autism, the question of whether or not to tell a child that he has autism is usually a moot point, because it is obvious he is different. However, many parents of children on the more able end of the spectrum struggle with the question of whether or not to tell their children that they have autism or Asperger's syndrome, or wonder at what age they should be told.

Many individuals who were diagnosed as adults report that the diagnosis gave them a starting point for looking for strategies to help themselves. Michael John Carley, the executive director of GRASP and author of *Asperger's from the Inside Out*, was diagnosed following the diagnosis of his son. Through his work at GRASP, the largest educational and advocacy organization in the world run by and serving adults along the autism spectrum, Michael often meets adults who have been recently diagnosed. He describes the most common response to be relief. Relief, because most of them knew they were different from everyone else, but did not know why. Now there is an explanation for why they are different, why they have always seemed to be walking to the beat of a different drum. Relief also because they knew where they could turn to support, meet other people like themselves, and find resources, when needed, to assist them in the areas that may present difficulties to them.

For those who were diagnosed following their child's diagnosis, they have a greater understanding of what their child is going through

---

PRACTICAL TIP

Providing examples of people who faced some of the same challenges yet are now happy and productive adults can be inspiring to your child. Everyone needs heroes to look up to. Sue Rubin and Tito Mukhopadhyay are people my son admires, and he enjoys hearing about them or seeing them at conferences. Knowing people like them have succeeded has made Jererny feel better about not being verbally fluent and having sensory motor challenges. There are many different types of people on the spectrum mentioned in this book and perhaps reading some of their writings to your child will inspire him as well.

---

and can help him while he is growing up to make sense of the world around him.

Dena Gassner was diagnosed at age thirty-eight and has a young adult son who has been diagnosed as being on the spectrum. As an autism consultant and from her involvement in autism organizations such as GRASP and the Autism Society of America, she meets many children and adults on the spectrum. She finds that the most successful adults are those who knew from the beginning that they were different, and why. Dena was misdiagnosed all through her childhood and adolescence, and feels she was "reborn" after her diagnosis as an adult. From Dena's experience, finding out she had autism led to questioning about what having autism meant for her, leading her to a better understanding of what supports she needed.

Dena feels strongly that parents who do not tell their children that they have autism or Asperger's syndrome are taking away their power. Dena likens being on the spectrum but not having a diagnosis to being in a wheelchair and having an office in a building that has no ramps or wheelchair access. Dena says that having a diagnosis is like moving to the building with the ramps—it may not be easy, but with the ramps you can find a way to get to your office and accomplish your work. For a child on the spectrum to be successful, he needs to be able to have those ramps, or tailored strategies to help him make sense of the world around him.

Dena observes that most of the parents of children on the spectrum

---

PRACTICAL TIP

To encourage a child to focus more on her positive attributes, talk to her about what you appreciate about her. If she is verbal or types, you can have a conversation and exchange opinions about your own positive attributes and areas of difficulty, as well as hers. If your child is not very communicative, hearing from you what you believe her strengths are and how much you enjoy her can still be helpful to building self-esteem.

---

she has met are somewhat different from parents of other special-needs children. For example, she has noticed that parents of children with Down syndrome go through a grief process and then continue on with making the most of their lives as a family, because it is clear what the child has and what caused this difference. Parents of children on the spectrum don't get a diagnosis right away; for many it takes a long time. For parents, there is often the loss of the child who develops normally, then regresses. Then, there is not one cause or reason to "blame" for the autism spectrum disorder. Some are still hoping for a cure or a recovery, and some parents of the more able children do not want to acknowledge there is a problem. For some or all of these reasons, parents stay on the grief cycle and take much longer to get over the diagnosis, which makes it harder to move forward and build those much-needed ramps.

Dena believes that for today's child on the spectrum, it is not just about teaching the child useful strategies to understand the neurotypical world, but also about encouraging our culture to be more accepting and understanding of differences. Dena also thinks that the goal of parents and teachers should not be to raise the children to be normal, but rather to teach them to manage their deficits. This means that they need a good dose of self-esteem as well as an ability to self-regulate. By learning to acknowledge the triggers they are experiencing as part of their autism and being able to manage their responses, they can become their own person, true to themselves.

Zosia Zaks, author of *Life and Love: Positive Strategies for Autistic*

FOOD FOR THOUGHT

WHY TELLING THE CHILD HE HAS
ASPERGER'S SYNDROME IS HELPFUL

Nick Dubin is the author of *Asperger Syndrome and Bullying: Strategies and Solutions*. Nick, who was diagnosed at age twenty-seven, has a master's degree in special education. For more information visit www.nickdubin.com.

I am firmly convinced that my self-esteem suffered during childhood and adulthood as a result of feeling "different" from everyone else. As clichéd as it might sound, growing up without a diagnosis does make you feel different. Labels are often described by people as "crutches," but in my case, receiving my diagnosis of Asperger's syndrome at the age of twenty-seven was the most liberating event of my life. Before the diagnosis, my neurological wiring confounded virtually everything I did. I couldn't multitask, stay organized, or tolerate surprises at all. I had a low "social quota," meaning that I got tired easily after socializing for a short period of time. These aspects of my personality befuddled me for twenty-seven years.

How does this relate to self-esteem? It relates because without having a neurological roadmap in the form of my Asperger's syndrome diagnosis, all of these peculiar behaviors went unexplained. As a result of that, I measured myself against the backdrop of everyone else. I saw that I operated in a certain way and everyone else apparently operated differently. I then began to view myself as being inferior to others because of these perceived and very real differences.

Aside from my own internalized shame, many teachers help to reinforce that shame, as well. For example, when I was in high school, I had a very uneven motor skill profile. As the number one singles player on my high school varsity tennis team, I obviously had very good gross motor skills. Yet during high school, I could not tie my own shoes, which meant that my fine motor skills were significantly behind. My teachers could not understand how such a fine tennis player could not even tie his own shoes. Using a "neurotypical" paradigm to explain this bizarre discrepancy, the theory was that I simply wasn't trying hard enough. Because of the faulty assumptions that several of my teachers made, they needlessly criticized me when I genuinely was trying. This in turn lowered my self-esteem greatly.[8]

Adults, was diagnosed at the age of thirty-one. When she was little, she was resistant to group activities and liked to do things over and over. While growing up, her parents were supportive of her in different ways. Academically, Zosia did well, thanks to her dad, who was able to help her by explaining what she needed to know. He also understood her sensory needs and did not talk at meals in restaurants, which made it easier for her. Mom was supportive of her in different ways, including accepting her inability to sit at the dinner table for too long. Yet there were still some expectations along the lines of, "If you are so smart academically, why can't you figure these things out?" A diagnosis of an autism spectrum disorder would have helped her understand why she was so competent academically yet nonetheless had many challenges.

When I met with Zosia, she explained that, while growing up, she wished she had had more of an understanding of the "why" behind things neurotypicals do or think, which they take for granted but which people on the spectrum do not naturally get. Zosia suggests to parents that it would be very helpful to explain out loud what people do as part of everyday "living"—for example, why we go to visit our grandparents, or the notion that most people do not know what they want to do when they go to college. This reminds me of the first time Jeremy and I took his assistant dog, Handsome, for a walk and I picked up after the dog. When we got home, Jeremy spelled out, "Mom why did you pick up Handsome's poop?" When I thought of it, it does seem like a really strange thing to do, but our society insists that we do this for reasons that are obvious to neurotypicals—so obvious we don't give them a moment's thought.

The Importance of a Few Good Friends or Mentors

Although we often think of children on the spectrum as being loners, most autistic adults talk about mentors and peers (on and off the spectrum) as well as their parents as being important factors in developing healthy self-esteem. Mentors can be teachers, therapists, relatives, or any person who takes a positive interest in the child and accepts him, warts and all. In previous chapters Brain King and others have described how uncomfortable they were in school environments for both sensory and social reasons. However, it is clear that many developed relationships with either autistic peers, nonautistic peers, teachers, or other mentors at school. It is these positive relationships that help students adapt to being a "stranger in a strange land," and encourages parents to continue sending their children to school despite other possible negative aspects.

The Need for a Peer Group

Kamran Nazeer was diagnosed early on with autism and attended a New York school for autistic children, a rarity in the early 1980s. In his book *Send in the Idiots: Stories from the Other Side of Autism*, he recounts the fate of some of his former classmates. Kamran's parents were scientifically minded and resourceful, and valued intelligence. When Kamran was around seven or eight and began to demonstrate how bright he was, showing an aptitude for math and reading, this made it easier for them to accept that he had autism and to be understanding of the behavior and social challenges he presented. Kamran has a sister who is three years younger, yet they grew up sort of like twins because he was at about the same developmental level she was. Kamran speaks very fondly of his sibling experience when young.

From Kamran's personal experience, he believes three factors are important to developing a strong sense of self-esteem and confidence. First and foremost is having accepting and supportive parents. Second is a relationship with an adult who is not a family member, such as a mentor or a therapist (as he had) who is not as emotionally involved. A more neutral person is needed, he says, because parents naturally display a sense of expectations, and it is important to have someone who is supportive of the child and accepting of the behavioral and social challenges. Third is access to a peer group who share the child's difficulties, who have the same struggles but are surviving as well. The class described in his book filled that role, although when he was growing up, Kamran didn't realize what an impact they had on his well-being. Kamran believes that although it is necessary for children to be mainstreamed, it is also essential not to feel as if you are the only one who faces the challenges presented by being on the autism spectrum.

How a Therapist Can Help

As it did for Kamran Nazeer, a one-on-one relationship with a therapist has also benefited Jordan Ackerson, a personable young man who graduated in 2006 with a modified high school diploma and attends a community college. When asked what has contributed to building up his self-esteem, he says there is always room for improvement in that area, but having people in his life who care very much about him, as well as caring about teaching him well, has been the key ingredient. Jordan believes that having a positive attitude and realizing that whatever happens in life will just happen, and that he needs to deal with whatever happens, have been helpful in making him more self-confident.

Jordan's mother, Lisa Lieberman, author of *A Stranger Among Us: Hiring In-Home Support for a Child with Autism Spectrum Disorders and Other Neurological Differences*, tells me that Jordan was raised with the overarching goal of promoting a strong sense of self- and inner confidence. Lisa believes this is mainly accomplished by teaching our children to advocate effectively on their own behalf, in order to develop a sense of potency and influence in their world. Some of her suggestions are mentioned in Chapter 9, "Self-Advocacy."

Lisa feels strongly that providing Jordan with the opportunity to have a one-on-one relationship with a child therapist who could understand his unique needs as a person with autism was crucial. Jordan has seen this person on an ongoing basis for many years. According to Lisa, Jordan treasures these sessions, and it appears that he is using the time well to process the challenges and confusion of growing up in a culture that is largely unforgiving of differences. In my observations of the family, it is obvious that the parents are truly proud of their son, and that they look forward to seeing him evolve as an adult in his own right.

Nonautistic Peers Can Be a Blessing

Sometimes it is a nonautistic peer group that can make all the difference in developing self-esteem. Michael Crouch, the college postmaster at the Crown College of the Bible in Tennessee, says he learned to enjoy life and developed confidence by being around nonautistic girls and teenagers. As mentioned earlier, it was teenage girls who encouraged him to become a member of the teen choir, and then the college choir. Singing in the choir and following vocal exercises given to him by his speech class teacher not only helped his speaking and vocal abilities but also built up his self-esteem.

Supportive Teachers Are Great Mentors

Teachers can be a major influence in developing strong self-esteem. It is apparent in talking with Jack Donehey-Nykiel, a college student majoring in Islamic Studies, that he is not lacking in confidence. Jack was diagnosed with Asperger's syndrome when he was thirteen. His parents both studied and taught Spanish for years and instilled in Jack a passion for learning about other cultures at an early age. Jack was bilingual by the time he was two and a half and was learning German by the time he was three.

Jack credits his parents and some of his teachers, with whom he shared common interests, for his high level of self-esteem. These supportive teachers viewed his interests as passions to be pursued—as opposed to obsessions to be dismissed. Jack's mother, Maureen, says his confidence also comes from acknowledging his deficits yet constantly reminding him of his strengths. Maureen feels that humor has helped a lot over the years. Jack and Maureen give public talks to increase awareness of the potential and untapped talent that may be hidden inside those on the spectrum who are functionally challenged by everyday living.

Good teachers and the right school environment have been beneficial to Elijah Wapner, a high school student and the aspiring comedian who appeared in the MTV *True Life* episode "I Have Autism." He reports having had difficulties in some areas during elementary school. Then, his mother, Valerie Paradiz, author of *Elijah's Cup*, founded ASPIE, a school (since closed) that offered a nurturing environment for students with

---

PRACTICAL TIP

If possible, find a trusted person who can be a mentor to your child when he is a teen. Having a caring teacher, coach, or therapist who connects with your teen and helps him mature into a young adult is a gift to be treasured. This adult can connect with your teen in a way that, as a parent, may not always be possible for you. Those lessons you as a parent have been trying to teach him—to make healthy choices, take responsibility for his actions, and do his best to reach his potential (no matter how high or how low)—are important things that every teen needs to hear reinforced by someone else besides his parents. Knowing that another adult believes in him, cares about him, and is there for him can be a life-saver for the autistic individual during his turbulent adolescent years.

Asperger's syndrome, and Elijah became more confident. Elijah credits his parents and his teachers at ASPIE for his healthy self-esteem, as they were always encouraging and cared about him. The people who were close to him when he was growing up all shared enthusiasm in his main interests, which was also important to his positive development.

Conclusion

The overall factors we know to be important in developing high self-esteem are: acceptance of the child, high expectations on the part of parents and teachers, and an emphasis on a child's strengths. Acceptance can come from a wide range of people—parents, teachers, family members, peers on or off the spectrum, and therapists. Severely impacted children who are able to overcome their difficulties have usually had the support of at least one person who had high expectations and put the time and effort into teaching them to overcome some of their challenges. Children who were less impacted and who developed high self-esteem had at least one person who realized they had deficits, but emphasized their strengths to help them become confident.

5

Pursuing Interests: The All-Important Art of Having Fun

TEACHER: *What do you like to do for fun?*

JEREMY: *I like to walk my dog. I like my friends to hang out.*

TEACHER: *What are your hobbies and interests?*

JEREMY: *Read about baseball in the newspaper, earning money, job would be nice. My interest is learning. It does not matter where.*

TEACHER: *Are there any school activities you would like to get involved in?*

JEREMY: *I like to go to dog group. I want to be in joking class.*

TEACHER: *Is there anything you wish you could learn to do that you don't know how?*

JEREMY: *I want to learn about joking. Baseball, write about baseball. Tell my story.*

—Allan Gustafson, interview with Jeremy Sicile-Kira,
spring 2007

When Jeremy was little, he loved following the patterns of our rugs or the intricate tile designs in the Paris apartment foyers over and over again. He loved spinning tops and Chinese soup spoons and would do it for hours if left to his own devices. It used to upset me; I was afraid he was too much in his own world, blocking us out. I thought I had to find a way to get him to connect with the world by playing "appropriately." Often I would try to join in with what he was doing to try to connect with him; other times I tried to teach him "fun" activities, how to use toys the way they were "supposed to" be used. We tried to get him engaged in our world, in our way.

When he got a little older, we had a behaviorally based home program and we taught him turn-taking table games. We also taught him to kick a ball back and forth to someone else, how to play catch, how to ride a bike, how to swim. We used behavioral methods to teach him. All this teaching took an enormous amount of time and energy, on his part as well as ours, because of his gross and fine motor challenges, sensory processing difficulties, and the social aspect that did not come naturally to him.

Although he tried and dutifully complied, of all the activities we taught him, swimming and doing wooden puzzles were the only activities he ever really got interested in and ever asked for. Even those activities were done in his "stimmy" way. He didn't swim—he floated or splashed or sank down to touch the line at the bottom of the pool with his foot. He dropped the pieces of the wooden puzzle a few times to hear the wonderful noise they made when they hit the table before putting the puzzle pieces in their places. However, all the activities we enticed him to participate in did help him with his eye-hand coordination, fine and gross motor skill, and sensory processing. They also taught him skills he needs today, such as waiting one's turn in line and water safety.

Nowadays, as a family we manage to find some things to do together that we all consider fun: going for walks and swims at the beach, having family and close friends over and enjoying good food with them, listening to music, going to the movies. Jeremy likes to walk his dog and hang out with friends. Hanging out with friends (the few he has) really just means being in the same space with them, or having them read to him and discussing via litewriter what was read, or listening to music with them, perhaps taking the dog to the beach together.

Jeremy still likes to look at patterns, but most of the time, the patterns are in a guitar magazine or in *Rolling Stone* or on the cover of *The New Yorker*. Sometimes he still plunks his old puzzle pieces. He pretty much just hangs out and stims whenever he can. However, it doesn't bother me anymore, because he spends a lot of time learning during the day, and he needs his down time. From what he communicates to people, I know he is "engaged" in the world. Jeremy mentions baseball as an interest, because his teacher, Allan, really likes baseball, so they read about baseball in the newspaper together, and that is how Jeremy connects to Allan. Jeremy is good at numbers and likes to write (in short spurts because it takes lot of work), but we are still waiting for that "special talent" to come popping through.

When he's asked, "learning" seems to be what he is really interested in. For most of us, that doesn't come under the rubric of fun, but I don't think his idea of fun is the same as for the rest of us. But that's okay. Who wouldn't want a teenager who says his main interest is learning? If he is out in the evening with a friend (a rare occasion), I don't have to worry about where he is, what he is doing, and if whoever is driving has been drinking. I know he is in good hands and is trying the best he can to engage in the world.

Pursuing Interests *Is* Having Fun

When I first met Zosia Zaks, author of *Life and Love: Positive Strategies for Autistic Adults*, one of the things we talked about was how she (and others on the spectrum) did not grasp the notion of "having fun." For many on the spectrum, activities are purpose-driven or interest-driven and the notion of doing something just because it feels good, passes the time of day, or makes you happy is not an obvious or appealing one. Zosia told me that she had no idea that there were activities people participated in just to have fun, and that as a child she did not realize she was supposed to be "having fun." It was one of those things about neurotypical living no one ever explained to her. Indeed, in her book, there is no chapter about recreational activities or hobbies.

In *Asperger's from the Inside Out* by Michael John Carley, "Intense absorption in a topic or field of interest" is listed as a characteristic of Asperger's syndrome. The negative interpretation of this characteristic is "Individual is obsessed, and is driven further into this absorption by anxiety and stress," whereas a more positive one is "Individual is passionate." In his book, Michael talks about how people on the spectrum often experience an extreme difficulty in focusing on topics or activities that do not interest them.

It is important to try to teach children on the spectrum appropriate play skills as a way of connecting with other children. Besides, there are other benefits from teaching appropriate play or what nonautistic children consider fun, such as turn taking and better eye-hand coordination. However, we need to give autistic children the time and space to do what they consider fun. Many parents and professionals spend an exorbitant amount of time, money, and energy trying to get children on the spectrum involved in what we nonautistic individuals think of as fun. Then they spend just as much time, money, and energy trying to get them to be less obsessive (positive translation: passionate) about whatever their special interest is. These special interests are varied and differ for each child, but include bus schedules, trains, astronomy, building structures, construction vehicles, numbers, detailed drawings of architectural monuments or cities, maps, historical facts, sports statistics, and military strategy.

For parents, it is hard to face the reality that your child doesn't enjoy the same activities you did as a child. As parents, we want to connect with our children, and we hope to do that by sharing with them the pleasure of the activities we used to enjoy as a child. Usually, men who played sports in school want their children to enjoy it as they did, and they want to bond with their sons in this way. Perhaps a mom enjoyed ballet and hopes her daughter will, too. The thing to remember is that even if your child were neurotypical, she might not be interested in the same things you enjoyed as a child. The important thing this is to find a way to connect and to bond with the children we have, and as the parents, we have to make the effort and find a way to do so, and put our personal disappointments aside, even though it is not always easy.

It is one thing to encourage a child to also focus on necessary subjects in order to make it through school and earn a diploma. However, more care should be taken when thinking about making children focus on what nonautistics consider "fun" activities—for the purpose of fun—that aren't fun for them. Team sports are difficult for many because of the sensory issues, as discussed in Chapter 1, and the social or communication difficulties. So are group activities such as Boy Scouts and Girl Scouts. Some children don't like painting or playing with modeling clay because they don't like the feel of the materials. Many children on the spectrum like to watch the same television programs over and over and are not interested in viewing new shows or going to the movies with the rest of the family. What is important is that we don't destroy their ability to be passionate, because this will help them in the future for possible career choices, and it will help them lead a life of fulfillment.

Most nonautistic adults have a hard time realizing that being passionate (neurotypical translation: obsessive) and engaging in a topic of interest is an autistic child's way of having fun. The great part is that they could eventually earn a living with their "special interest." The child who loves bus schedules can end up being the information contact at a bus terminal. The child who is gifted at making detailed drawings of cities can become a map or book illustrator. The child who is passionate about construction vehicles may enjoy working in some form of the construction industry or learn to repair construction equipment. Of course, not every obsessive thing a child on the spectrum does is proof of an inner talent or has the makings of a thriving future career, but if we are just looking at the "fun factor," we need to see this from their point of view, without judgment, and try to engage in or be supportive of their fun.

What Many Nonautistic People Like to Do for Fun: An Alternative Perspective

Before discussing children on the spectrum, just for fun (did I really write that?), let's make a list of activities that are usually considered enjoyable, recreational activities by many nonautistic adults.

- Spending hours sitting on a hard seat in the cold/heat/rain, in a noisy, crowded, smelly environment with greasy food, watching men (usually) run after each other doing something that involves a ball (going to a live football, basketball, baseball, or soccer match at a big stadium).

- Spending three or four hours chasing a little ball with a big stick around a big green park in all kinds of weather, and paying lots of money for the pleasure of doing so (golf).
- Spending Sunday afternoons and Monday nights with other grown-ups drinking beer and watching men in spandex run around a field with a blown-up piece of pigskin (Sunday/Monday night football on television).
- Spending hours in crowded environments with loud music and too much lighting to bring home stuff that will just sit in your already crowded closet most of the time and increase the amount of your debt (shopping).
- Spending hours in a smelly, brightly lit environment and paying money to someone to put chemicals on your fingernails and toenails and then having to wait for the chemicals to dry before you can use your hands again or put your shoes back on and leave (getting your nails done).
- Spending hours in a crowded, noisy environment and spending money on beverages that make you act silly, lose all inhibitions, and prevent you from driving yourself home (hanging out at a bar and drinking alcohol).
- Spending time and lots of money to be served delicious food and expensive wines that will soon be but a memory, and that our bodies will eliminate within a few hours, all served by tidy and judgmental people wearing uniforms (frequenting expensive restaurants).

You get the picture. If someone landed here from another planet, they wouldn't really understand why these things are fun. We would appear weird to them.

Here in San Diego there is a beautiful Model Railroad Museum that has miles of wonderful train tracks with models of all different types of trains. I used to take my children there when they were little. One day we walked into the museum and saw a group of grown men, dressed in rail-

---

PRACTICAL TIP

Observe what activities your child seems to like doing, then join in with him. Creating a bond with your child, and having fun his way, is a good way to get him interested in you. Then you can try to introduce new elements to what the two of you are doing together. Perhaps he will enjoy the time together and be open to trying something you like, and discover more neurotypical play skills along the way. But if not, at least you will have strengthened your bond and spent time with him, and that is essential.

---

road outfits, playing with the trains. They turned out to be a club of model railroad enthusiasts, and they would meet on a regular basis at the museum and keep up the trains there, and run them. I did not have the opportunity to chat with them, but immediately thought of a few people (children and adults) on the spectrum who would be happy to spend some time there. It looked a little weird, but not really any weirder than some activities described above.

Some people on the spectrum have mentioned (see Chapter 2, "Communication") that they don't "get" idle chitchat. Perhaps what neurotypicals see as "having fun" is really another version of idle chitchat: it passes the time, but it doesn't really get anywhere. Some may argue that fun activities are a way of bonding with other people, and that may be true, but an activity only serves the purpose of bonding if the people involved are enjoying it. Mainly, we do these things because they give us pleasure. And if we don't get pleasure out of it, what is the point?

I have never liked beer. I am a wine drinker. I have been told that beer is an acquired taste. When I was in college, I tried to acquire a taste for beer. I figured that if so many people enjoy beer, there must be a reason. I have lived and visited countries that are known for their excellent beers and have tried them. I still don't like beer. My point is, does it matter that I don't like beer? Why should I spend time acquiring a taste for something I don't like just because most people do? The same goes for "fun" activities we try to teach autistic children.

What Some Children and Adults
on the Spectrum Like to Do for Fun

What do people on the spectrum like to do for fun? If you've ever attended a national conference put on by the Autism Society of America (ASA), you would know that some adults and teens on the spectrum find dancing to music and splashing in the pool at night to be fun. I know because I have seen the little rubber duckie floating in the pool when I go for my early-morning swim, which is probably a lot less fun than splashing about with a bunch of people you like in the middle of the night. I have been involved in some of the dancing, and I will tell you it is fun dancing with people on the spectrum because they are uninhibited— they don't care about how they look or whether they have the right moves, they are just enjoying the music. How refreshing!

It may surprise many people to know that Sue Rubin (*Autism Is a World*) likes to go to the racetrack. She doesn't live far away from one of the most well-known racetracks, and this is a fun thing she does on a regular basis. (I haven't asked her if she is good at picking horses. If she is, I see a new career developing as a handicapper.)

DJ Savarese (*Reasonable People*) likes to "give my dad the sign for fearless tickling" and also is the only person in Iowa with his own trampoline house. DJ and his family used to live in Florida, and DJ's great pleasure (besides getting tickles from his dad), and a way of connecting to people, was to jump on this big outdoor trampoline. When his father, Ralph, accepted a teaching position at Grinnell College, they had to move to Iowa, where the local weather does not lend itself to outdoor trampolines on a year-round basis. So Ralph built a structure in their yard just for the trampoline.

According to Jasmine Lee O'Neill, a mute autistic savant and author of *Through the Eyes of Aliens*, there are many activities an autistic child can enjoy. Contrary to what most people think, they are able to play; it is just a different type of playing than what nonautistic children do. Many like to run, roll around, jump, tumble, and whirl. Children on the spectrum need to stay fit like any other child, and some have lots of energy to expend. Some children enjoy horseback riding and nature. Jamie suggests looking closely at what the child enjoys doing and encouraging those activities. Some who like geography can spend time looking at maps and connecting with others over that. A child who likes to collect rocks might enjoy visiting a science museum. The key to finding fun or recreational activities is to look at what the child enjoys.

Childhood Interests and Developing Talents for the Future

There are many children and teens on the spectrum who do not have particular talents or passions, or if they do, we have not discovered them yet. But for those who do, these interests or passions could very well turn into the basis of a career or a way to earn some money as an adult. Meanwhile, we can use the object of their passion to teach children what they need to learn in school or at home.

Temple Grandin often speaks to audiences about the need to build on a child's strengths and to use their special interests to teach necessary concepts. For example, if a child is fascinated by trains, you can build lessons around trains. Trains can be used to teach concepts of color and basic math as well as geography and more. As the child gets older, he can use trains to tackle more difficult math problems and learn about the different types of engines (steam, combustion, etc.) and how they run. Economics can be taught, and so on, all centered around trains. Eventually this special interest can be used to help figure out a possible career as a train engineer or train conductor.

With the unemployment rate as high as it is for those on the spectrum, we need to ensure that we don't snuff out any possibility they may have of a marketable skill. According to the 2002 report by the President's Commission on Excellence in Special Education, unemployment rates have hovered at around 70 percent for disabled adults for the last twelve years. In the United Kingdom, estimates of unemployed or underemployed adults on the spectrum are as high as 85 percent, according to the National Autistic Society. We need to be looking at how those who do have jobs managed to get them and keep them. In Chapter 10, you will find some examples of how early interests developed into careers

---

PRACTICAL TIP

Granted, for some it is easy to figure out right off the bat what they are good at and what they enjoy doing and how that applies to a possible career. For others it is not so easy. Perhaps keeping a journal, jotting down what you see your child doing, what activity he engages in when left to his own devices, can help you see other patterns emerging that can give you a clue as to a future area of interest to develop.

---

that have given autistic individuals satisfaction in adulthood as well as the potential to earn a living.

Temple Grandin recalls as a child that she absolutely hated dolls, but she loved building things. When she was around six or seven, her father used to get his shirts washed at a laundry service, and the shirts would come back folded around a piece of cardboard. Temple would take that shirt cardboard, adhesive tape, and a pair of scissors and build to her heart's content. She remembers once making an elaborate aircraft carrier, putting wood shingles on the roof, and making soldiers out of white adhesive tape. Temple went on to become famous for designing livestock-handling facilities, among many other accomplishments.

Author Stephen Shore was diagnosed with atypical development with strong autistic tendencies and was nonverbal until the age of four. He strongly believes in having fun, which is part of the reason he gives music lessons to children with autism. (In fact, he is usually the first one on the dance floor at the ASA national conferences.)

However, what is fun for someone on the spectrum is not necessarily what neurotypical children think of as fun. Stephen's idea of fun when he was growing up was taking apart and putting back together watches, clocks, and bicycles to see what made them work. This eventually led to a job in a bicycle shop, doing repairs. He loved going to yard sales to look for old tube radios to take apart. He enjoyed "dialoguing" with the old tube radios, meaning he used the dial to see how far away he could reach

AM radio stations. From where he lived in Massachusetts, he was able to tune into stations as far away as Salt Lake City to the west, Canada to the north, and Florida to the south. Once he was able to tune into a station in Holland!

Stephen's parents were very supportive of the activities that he found fun. For example, his father got him a booklet that listed the call letters for all the radio stations to help him with his dialoguing pursuit. They also gave him a chemistry set and installed a small makeshift chemistry bench in his bedroom to help him pursue his interest in chemistry. Stephen's mother shared some of the same interests he had, such as listening to different versions of the same piece of music. She had also been interested in astronomy when she was younger, so she was able to help him pursue that interest. Stephen enjoyed reading, and read the whole encyclopedia from A to Z. To this day, he still enjoys reading three or four books concurrently.

Stephen enjoyed riding his bicycle, yet found most "age-appropriate" toys boring. The only things he liked to play with were Legos, but he played with them in an autistic fashion: in those days, Legos were in red and white only, and he always built in alternating red and white patterns. Teen sports held no attraction to him because he had difficulty dealing with nonverbal behavior and he had motor planning challenges.

Stephen suggests that parents and teachers should encourage children to have fun, but fun means what the *child* enjoys doing, not the nonautistic adult's idea of fun. Besides helping a child to connect with the adult and to enjoy life, the adult will also be helping the child lay the groundwork for possible future careers to pursue.

Daniel Tammet, author of *Born on a Blue Day*, writes that when he was a child, books became very important to him, and he would drag his parents' books up to his room and hoard them. He would sort the books into piles that no one was allowed to move without risking an outburst from Daniel. He felt happy surrounded by the books, as the pages all had numbers on them and he felt wrapped in a numerical security blanket. Long before he could read the sentences on the pages, he could count the numbers that appeared to him in colored shapes or in motion in his mind.

Jack Donehey-Nykiel, the young Islamic Studies student mentioned in Chapter 4, has always been interested in languages and other cultures. He was bilingual by the time he was two and a half, and was learning German by the time he was three. As he got older, he taught himself Italian because he developed an interest in Dante. During his elementary school years he became an expert in epidemiology and then studied the tribes of Africa. In his early years at school the teachers were amazed and puzzled by his giftedness, and Jack shares that a few of them saw his interests as a problem and tried to suppress them. Relationships with his peers were difficult as they were intrigued by Jack's knowledge on a variety of unusual subjects yet confused at his lack of comprehension of the "hidden curriculum," or unspoken set of social norms and expectations, and so he was at times bullied. More supportive teachers encouraged Jack to ignore the students who were attacking him and making fun of his interests.

Jack is working toward completing his degree in Islamic Studies, and I wish him every success. The world needs more people with an understanding of that part of the world. Perhaps he will be a professor, or perhaps he will be a diplomat. At any rate, he will be a credit to his parents, who are a good source of support and encouragement for him. His mother, Maureen Donehey, a high school Spanish teacher, holds a master's degree in linguistics and another in educational administration, and is a special education consultant. She has given him essential encouragement to pursue his passions, from a young age.

Michael Crouch, college postmaster at the Crown College of the Bible, clearly loves his job. His interest in delivering mail started at an early age. He recalls, "Mom gave me the joy of checking the mail. We lived out in the country at the time, off of a state highway. We got our property fenced in with the mailbox outside of it off the highway. Every time we came home for the day, I went out to open the gate (I actually had a key—the only key I actually used at the time), check the mail, and then close the gate! When we left to go somewhere, I would do the same!"

Elijah Wapner, the teenager who is working toward being a comedian, grew up in Woodstock, New York, which is famous for its rock

FOOD FOR THOUGHT

FOR PARENTS OF CHILDREN SEVERELY IMPACTED BY AUTISM:
HOW TO INTERPRET BEHAVIORS TO FIND THAT SPECIAL TALENT

Many of us parents of children severely impacted by autism still get comments from well-meaning people we meet out in public, "Oh, your child has autism. They are all so smart and have a special gift. What is your child's special talent?" Although I love my son and I know that he is smart, I don't really perceive a special talent. But perhaps I have not spent enough time interpreting his behaviors and favorite activities that may indicate a hidden talent that could lead to a profitable career. This realization led me to think about and create the following list of behaviors enjoyed by some of the children I know, along with my subjective interpretations—you may have your own. Perhaps you will find a clue to your child's inner talent. Or perhaps you will enjoy a few minutes of laughter, something we all need every now and then!

BEHAVIOR	FUTURE CAREER
Lines up toys	Professional organizer
Spins tops	Physics professor
Spins all objects	Physics researcher
Takes clothes off, will not leave them on	Director of a clothing-optional community
Hits people	Boxer
Twirls piece of string for hours	Wind velocity researcher
Dumps bags of sugar and flour	Competitor in adult sandcastle competition
Chews and swallows nonfood items (pica)	Food taster for a head of state
Runs around the house, will not sit down	Sprinter
Tries to escape the house or other enclosed area	Cross-country runner
Gets up on the furniture and jumps off	Parachutist or bungee jumper
Takes things apart but does not put them together again	Neurotypical husband

history. Music, particularly of the 1960s, 1970s, and 1980s, is one of Elijah's special interests. His other special interest is stand-up comedy and performance. When he was a child, he used to spend a lot of time memorizing and telling jokes from joke books. Now, Elijah writes his own material and does stand-up in some comedy clubs as well as at autism conferences. He is studying drama and stand-up comedy and takes classes at a prestigious studio in New York City.

Conclusion

Many of the activities that we nonautistic people consider fun are not interesting or appealing to children on the autism spectrum. Teaching traditional play activities that will help foster social contact, encourage sharing, and enhance gross and fine motor development is a good idea. However, we should try to engage with the child in whatever *she* considers fun in order to make a connection. Encouraging the child in her area of interest can be helpful for her future career as well as her current self-esteem. Many children can be taught what they need to know in school by using topics they are passionate about. Areas of interest can be the basis for social relationships, and mentors can help cultivate areas of interest into a useful future employment opportunity.

6

Self-Regulation

TEACHER: *What kind of supports do you think you need to help accomplish your goals?*

JEREMY: *I need people who will teach me what I need to know. I need help for my sensory problems.*

TEACHER: *How do you handle conflicts or solve problems?*

JEREMY: *My engines are high. I need help to help me.*

—Allan Gustafson, interview with Jeremy Sicile-Kira,
spring 2007

When Jeremy was little, he could sit for long periods of time, rocking himself and twirling anything he could get his hands on. By the time he got to junior high, though, he could manage sitting for only twenty minutes at a time. As a sophomore in high school, he had a tough time sitting through general education classes that lasted two hours. After about thirty minutes he would get up and bolt out of the room. Granted, two hours is a long time for any teenager to sit, but he needed to be able to stay sitting for longer periods of time if he was going to reach his goal of learning in general education classes in the local high school. He had to learn to communicate to his instructional aide his need to leave before he had a complete sensory breakdown, not just get up and rush out the door. He needed to learn to take sensory breaks—short periods of time away from the classroom lights and noise, doing activities that would help him refocus.

By the time he was a senior, Jeremy was able to sit for about an hour and fifteen minutes without the need for a sensory break. When he needed one, he would hand his instructional aide a "break card." Then, they would leave the classroom, go for a ten-minute walk to decompress, and then return to the classroom for the remainder of the lesson.

Recently Jeremy has been affected by a multitude of emotional feelings and changes in his environment and schedule that have made it difficult for him to self-regulate. His grandfather passed away, he changed schools and had to deal with a new environment and new classmates while missing his old ones, and he lost the occupational therapist who had helped him for years. All this has made it very hard for him to regulate his sensory and emotional overload. However, with the help of the aides and the Afternoon Angels (his tutors), an occupational therapist who worked with him before, and a psychologist, he is getting back on track. He is now back to monitoring his emotional and sensory state and regulating his responses to the events in his life. Even with the best-laid plans, real life happens—things we have no control over—and Jeremy has been learning to deal with these challenges in order to keep his progress on track.

Why Children Need to Learn to Self-Regulate

Self-regulation is a necessary life skill that all human beings need to practice. As discussed at length in Chapter 1, sensory processing difficulties are a real concern for children on the autism spectrum. Along with the challenge of trying to make sense of the world comes the related challenge of avoiding sensory overload. Emotionally as well, it is difficult for children on the spectrum to understand what they are feeling and how to control their emotional responses. No man is an island, and self-regulation is a necessary aspect of enjoying community life. If a toddler throws a temper tantrum, it is usually considered developmentally normal, but when he attends school, after a certain age such a display is inappropriate in a public setting. Eventually, little by little, children learn to manage their emotions as they get older. As discussed in Chapter 1, sensory or emotional overload can lead to real feelings of fear and anxiety, and children may experience their heart beating extremely fast. Learning to recognize that they are experiencing sensory or emotional overload and to regulate their response is a necessary but difficult lesson.

No matter what the level of impairment of the child on the spectrum, self-regulation is a skill that can be taught. The amount of time it takes and the methods used will vary depending on the child's age and ability level, as well as the reason she is having the sensory or emotional overload. Biomedical interventions, sensory integration techniques, social stories, cognitive behavioral therapy, behavior modification, communication, deep pressure, and a squeeze machine—these and various other methods have been used to help people on the spectrum learn to self-regulate.

All children need to learn to take responsibility for their behavior. For those children who are verbal and impulsive, they must learn to think before they speak as their honesty will get them into trouble. Teenagers on the spectrum who are fully integrated will find it difficult and will face unwanted consequences for not learning to control their impulsivity, their emotions, and their sensory overloads.

By the time they reach the adult years, if they have not learned to self-regulate and have not replaced inappropriate behaviors with more appropriate ones, it will be very hard for them to be mainstreamed in society, have friends, hold jobs, attend college, or live independently or in a supported living situation. It will be difficult for them to take part in community life without eventually creating bad feelings in others or, more tragically, getting themselves into trouble with the law. I believe that society needs to be more accepting of nonneurotypical people, but there are some rules of good manners that everyone should try to follow.

Self-Awareness

Before a child can learn to control her responses to an environment that is overwhelming her, she needs to understand what she is feeling and what it means. She needs to have a certain amount of self-awareness. Self-awareness is all about being able to recognize what different emotions look and feel like in yourself and in others, and being able to recognize when you are about to have an emotional breakdown. For those on the spectrum, it's also about being able to recognize how your body is feeling and what is causing sensory overload, and to recognize what it feels like *before* a meltdown is going to occur so that you can learn what works to calm your system down.

Zosia Zaks, author of *Life and Love: Positive Strategies for Autistic Adults*, describes the difficulties of recognizing the physical feelings of "I'm hungry" and emotions such as "I'm lonely." She says she had to learn what these feelings and emotions were, and that she was capable of making them go away by taking the necessary steps.

As discussed in previous chapters, children on the spectrum are not good at picking up on body language, including facial expressions. A young child can be taught, using visual representations as well as verbal descriptions and modeling, what the different emotions look like—happy, sad, angry, and so on. Then she can begin to identify the emotions in real life, both in herself as well as others. She can also learn to describe (verbally or with pointing) the intensity of emotions on a scale of 1 to 5. This helps her both understand and communicate not just the emotion itself but also how strongly it is being experienced and expressed.

Dena Gassner, MSW, who was diagnosed as an adult, believes it is necessary for children to be able to identify what their "triggers" are. It is important for parents, family members, and those working with the child to affirm to the child that whatever she is feeling is important. Even if it does not make sense to you or to others, whatever the child is feeling is true for her.

In addition, besides learning to recognize their emotional state, children need to recognize what "speed" their engine is running at. My son

Jeremy's special education teacher asked him every day about how he was feeling and where he was on a 1 to 5 scale. If he was a 3, that was good—relatively calm. Jeremy learned through experience and the teacher's explanation that if he was a 4, he was heading for sensory overload, and he had to do something to get back down to a 3 or he would have a hard time focusing on work. This discussion every day helped Jeremy recognize what he was feeling. By becoming aware of what his body felt like *before* reaching the point of overload, Jeremy could become proactive and take a sensory break before reaching the overload state.

Self-Regulation

Self-regulation refers to the body's ability to sense needs and, for the most part, address them. This means that if your internal temperature is too hot, your body will begin to sweat; when your body is dehydrated, it will start craving water; and so on. Consciously, self-regulation consists of the choices that we make when we feel cold or hungry, sleepy, and so on. To be able to self-regulate, a certain amount of self-awareness is needed. For example, young children will often say, "My tummy hurts," but they can't identify whether it is because their bladder is full and they need the restroom, or because their stomach is hungry and they need to eat. As their body matures, and so do they, they learn to recognize the difference. Then, they learn to eat when they are hungry and go to the restroom when they recognize the feeling of a full bladder. This is an example of how neurotypical children learn. For some children on the spectrum, the ability to self-regulate can take a long time to develop.

For those who suffer from sensory or emotional overload, coping techniques will help them learn to get their overloads under control. For example, blogger and advocate Amanda Baggs faces severe processing challenges. When I asked her about self-regulation, Amanda described how she had to learn that unless she was doing something harmful to herself or to other people, then whatever her body chose to do was probably what needed to happen. If she let go of trying to keep her body still in one spot, then her body would move in a way that drastically reduced her overload and increased her comprehension level.

PRACTICAL TIP

Teaching children over time to recognize their emotional state as well as how they are feeling before an overload takes place is the first step in giving them the tools to practice self-regulation. Finding the kinds of activities that they can do in a sensory break to help get regulated is the second step. Then, they can learn to communicate the need for a sensory break in an appropriate manner, which should be respected. Cognitive behavioral therapy, which encourages the cognitive control of emotions, can be useful for many.

Amanda has learned that she can carry objects that have a familiar texture and shape in order to handle other changes more readily. She also learned it was okay to go lie down or do something repetitive when she needed a break. Amanda says that the times she really would fall apart was when she had no breaks in between being expected to process a lot of new information. She learned that these breaks are just as important to autistic people as sleep is to neurotypicals, and that perhaps they need more time for the less conscious part of the brain to filter through the information while they are doing something else. For everyone, that "something else" is different—for some it is reading, for others it could be playing with blocks, for others zoning out.

For Jeremy, the overload in the general education classroom results from trying to process the lecture material he is hearing while sitting under bright lights and hearing other background noise. He can't tune out the other noise and just focus on the teacher's voice; he hears this all the same. As explained earlier, he learned to recognize when he was headed for sensory overload. Then he learned to communicate to his aide by handing her a "break card" when he could feel he was getting to that point. They would leave the classroom for a sensory break—a brisk ten-minute walk outside. Eventually the goal is for him to find things he can do while in the class without disrupting his classmates that will help ward off an impending overload and the need to leave class at all.

Many children on the spectrum who tantrum or bolt to "get out of work," as is sometimes thought, might really be suffering from sensory or emotional overload and be needing a break. Teaching them over time to recognize their emotional state and how they are feeling before a sensory overload occurs can give them the opportunity to be able to communicate the need for a break (which should be respected). Of course, you don't want your child or student to learn he can get out of work anytime he feels like it by bolting out the door. However, if you take data over a one-week or two-week period, you can determine how long the child seems to be able to work before trying to get away. Then, you can give him a break before he gets overloaded and bolts, and he can be rewarded for sitting and working. He is not getting reinforced for bolting out the door. Eventually, you can increase by small increments the amount of time he is sitting, and he will be able to handle a sensory overload because he will know a break is coming.

Because of the sensory challenges she faces, Zosia Zaks has come up with a Sensory Emergency Kit. In her book, *Life and Love*, she suggests personalizing this kit and carrying it around for whenever needed. Zosia has included some suggestions for what to include, such as sunglasses or a visor to shade the eyes from light, an iPod or Walkman, earplugs or noise cancellation earphones to drown out sound, a personal filtration mask to filter out smells (or how about cotton balls seeped in a favorite scent?), tolerable snacks and drinks, gum or candy, distraction items (little puzzles, games, pad and pencil), tactile items to hold or squish or roll to soothe the child, and extra clothes for temperature issues.

In Chapter 1, Brian King discussed how sensory processing challenges affect him. He describes sensory overload as being when he has reached the point of neurological saturation. Brian says that sensory breaks to decompress are very helpful, yet hard to fit into the kind of work he is doing right now. For him, an effective sensory break is to go to his room and block out all light and sound until he recovers. Brian also discussed with me how much of the school day, especially when he reached junior high, was spent wondering where the next sensory assault would come from.

Sensory overload was particularly challenging for him in junior high. This is traditionally when students start to have different classrooms and different teachers, and are required to negotiate hallways full of other

FOOD FOR THOUGHT

LEARNING TO SELF-REGULATE

Jordan Ackerson is a personable young man on the spectrum who graduated in 2007 with a modified high school diploma and is attending a community college. His mother is Lisa Lieberman, author of *A Stranger Among Us: Hiring In-Home Support for a Child with Autism Spectrum Disorders and Other Neurological Differences*. This is how Jordan describes his efforts to self-regulate:

Counseling has been very useful. I started out doing more play therapy than talking at the beginning of 5th grade when I was 11. Now I spend the whole hour talking and I always have a lot to discuss. The reason I find it helpful is because it helps me to talk about things so that I feel more confident about myself as a teenager. I just wish more teenagers could have counseling because it's also common for them to feel like they're struggling in life. I am in the process of learning some skills in how to self-soothe. For example, one night I was regretting something I had done. I tried to use self-talk to reassure myself that it wasn't as big of a deal as it felt emotionally, at the time. Also, deep breathing can help me deal with frustration and feel more relaxed, as a result. I have learned that a lot of places are going to have some loud and sudden noises. I can tolerate twice as much exposure to loud sound as I've matured. I had a lot of sensory integration therapy when I was younger which I am sure helped me to not feel so uncomfortable in the sensory environment.

students going every which way. Lights, noise, touch—all of it was just too much for Brian's sensory system whenever he had to change classes. He remembers reaching his English classroom every day saying, "Thank God I got here!" He spent most of his schooltime hyperfocused on waiting for the next sensory assault. Brian says that most students as sensitive as he is spend their time in school just trying to make it through the day. Many parents have recounted how their child holds it together at school and then has a meltdown when he gets home, and teachers report more meltdowns at the end of the school day.

PRACTICAL TIP

Teaching your child a way to communicate his or her sensory discomfort will make life easier for everyone. Be aware of how your child responds to self-care routines such as brushing teeth or combing her hair. Does she seem to be avoiding these routines because it is too physically painful? Finding ways to desensitize those highly sensitive areas can be very helpful. An experienced occupational therapist can help in this area.

For Sue Rubin, it was learning a way to communicate that helped her to have more and more control over self-injurious behaviors such as head banging and scratching. Behaviors toward others included yelling and biting. In her presentations over the past years, Sue shares that when she was little, she was unable to control her behaviors, and that quite a bit of her inability to learn was due to behaviors getting in the way of her ability to focus. Often the behaviors were in response to sensory issues, such as getting her haircut or her teeth cleaned. Sue remembers being abusive toward the hairdresser and the dentist as a child. Sometimes these behaviors were brought on by rages. Sue points to behavior modification, planning, and learning to communicate as the methods she has used to better control her behaviors. In addition, her parents, teachers, therapists, and others who worked with her when she was growing up learned how to spot these behaviors early and de-escalate them before it was too late.

Nick Dubin, author of *Asperger Syndrome and Bullying*, recounts that when he was three or four, he hyperactively flapped his arms continuously and jumped up and down with boundless energy, and needed a lot of physical movement to stay regulated. His parents were concerned about the nonstop motor activity. Even when he was of school age, he still needed to jump and flap to stay regulated. He would jump up and down in the classroom, calling attention to himself and inviting many stares. By the age of nine or ten, he was diagnosed with attention deficit hyperactivity disorder (ADHD) because in those days people were unfamiliar with Asperger's syndrome and its typical regulation issues.

PRACTICAL TIP

Take a good look at your child's behaviors over a two-week period and record data on any acting-out behaviors. Make notes on what happened before the behavior took place (antecedent), what happened during the behavior, and what happened after (the consequence). See if you can find a pattern as to whether the behavior is a result of sensory overload, or is as Temple would call it, just "bad behavior." This way, you will have a better idea of how to help the child best, whether it be linking behavior to consequences and following through or finding an appropriate way to regulate sensory issues.

Donna Williams credits her ability to self-regulate in part to sticking to a diet to curtail the severe food allergies that affect her behavior, as mentioned in Chapter 1. Donna has used biomedical interventions such as nutritional and vitamin supplements and has been on gluten-free/casein-free, low-salicylate, low-sugar diets for more than a decade. Strict adherence to the diet is extremely helpful to keep Donna's behaviors in check. Gluten is a plant protein found in wheat, oats, barley, and rye, and in some autistic individuals, it is incompletely broken down to form neurotoxic substances. The same is true for casein, a protein found in cow's milk, and it also causes digestive problems in some people. Salicylates are chemical compounds found in many fruits, flavorings, drugs, and household products. Aspirin, for example, contains salicylates. Some autistic individuals are adversely affected by ingesting foods and substances containing these chemicals.

Behaving Appropriately

Temple Grandin believes that it is never too early to implement good, sound parenting strategies in the home and to establish expectations for appropriate behavior. However, she says that parents and teachers need to be able to tell the difference between bad behavior, which deserves a consequence, and behaviors that are due to sensory overload or some other autism-related challenge. In the latter cases, it is appropriate intervention, not behavioral consequences, that will help. For example, she believes regular exercise can have a calming effect on some people who may be anxious or too hyper. Some may find wearing hats with brims and sunglasses helpful for preventing overload from fluorescent lights, or earplugs helpful for avoiding auditory overload.

Jerry Newport, author of *Your Life Is Not a Label*, and coauthor with his wife, Mary, of *Autism-Asperger's & Sexuality* and *Mozart and the Whale*, says that children on the spectrum have many reasons for growing into angry teens and angrier adults. However, having an autism spectrum disorder is not an excuse for emotionally or physically destructive behaviors, and those who feel angry need to learn anger management skills. Jerry has found the "three-second rule" helpful. Whereas before Jerry would impulsively respond to an unpleasant situation, he now waits three seconds, realizes he is still alive, and recognizes that perhaps it is not so bad after all.

In Chapter 8, "Social Relationships," we will look at appropriate and inappropriate behaviors in a social context.

Conclusion

Learning self-awareness is a necessary precursor to mastering self-regulation. Children need to recognize emotions in themselves and others as well as to recognize their tolerance levels for sensory overload. Various methods can be used to help them become self-aware, including visual and verbal descriptions of emotional states, using a scale from 1 to 5, and ample practice in identifying the emotions when they occur in the child and in others. Children need to be taught alternative acceptable behaviors and encouraged to take breaks rather than having meltdowns. Learning to communicate the need for a break *before* a tantrum is a good goal, as is learning techniques for self-soothing. As children get older, cognitive behavioral therapy can also help them learn to self-regulate.

7

Independence

TEACHER: *What kind of chores do you like to do at home?*
JEREMY: *Clean my room, set table.*

TEACHER: *Are there any areas in your personal life in which you have
   difficulties?*
JEREMY: *Yes, Fridays, moving, cooking at house, cutting. Mom is great with
   my difficulties. No more great difficulties.*

TEACHER: *If you moved to a new community tomorrow,
   what could you do without help?*
JEREMY: *Take off my shoes and clothes and put on my shoes and clothes.*

—Allan Gustafson, interview with Jeremy Sicile-Kira,
spring 2007

Jeremy wants to have his own house with roommates, good
friends, and a fun job and to continue learning. Jeremy does not
talk in years; such as he wants it now or in ten years. He does not
know and trusts that mom will know when the time is right. He
worries about if there will be people to help him to continue to

learn and to help him cope with the environment. Jeremy knows he needs help, and wants to help his family by saving money so he can do things he would not be able to do by himself.

—Allan Gustafson, interview with Jeremy Sicile-Kira,
spring 2007

Independence has always been difficult for Jeremy. Because of his sensory processing challenges and fine and gross motor difficulties, it has been hard for him to learn basic skills that require coordination of any kind. I have had the help of many professionals over the years, but I have had to figure things out myself in order to teach Jeremy certain everyday skills. Take, for example, fastening his pants. Jeremy could button his pajama tops, a skill we had taught him over some months, but fastening the button on blue jeans and other pants was a different fine motor sequence (try it and you will see). It was as if his fingers could not respond. It took a combination of discrete trial teaching, prompts and rewards, and modifying the different materials we were working with (nothing in the catalogs helped) to get to the point where he could fasten the button on his jeans by himself. It took years.

Chores that did not involve fine motor skills seem to be easier for him. He can empty the dishwasher and do a load of laundry with minimal assistance. We have discovered that he is good at math and can use his math skills to figure out how much he needs to save to be able to buy a particular item, and he can do a rudimentary business plan. No matter how difficult, though, he is expected to participate in household chores (not enough, though, as far as his sister Rebecca is concerned).

He still needs help in most areas and is far from self-sufficient. However, this year has seen a major shift in Jeremy and his independence. Whereas in the past he would drag me to the fridge and ask for things, he now attempts to get food out himself. He has gotten better about being able to pull things out without knocking other items out of the fridge and onto the floor. This morning, Jeremy pulled me to the fridge and then spelled out, "I need you to help me get some food." He was not asking for me to do something for him; he was asking me to assist while he tried to help himself. I treasure steps forward such as this. It might not sound like much, but it represents a great deal of progress and an important mind-set of doing things for himself.

Independence Looks Different for Everyone

Zosia Zaks remarked to me that parents of children with autism need to realize and accept that they will be parenting for a lot longer than parents of neurotypical children. She has a point, but I never thought I'd still be discussing toileting issues when my son was old enough to vote!

It is important to note that many adults on the spectrum are still improving themselves and their essential skills, and that for many, some of the skill acquisition came later in life. This is nice to know because so often as parents we hear about "windows of opportunity" in terms of age and often we are discouraged by some pessimistic professionals, uncharitable acquaintances, and our own inner cynics ("Well, if he hasn't learned it by now . . . "). It is a good idea to start early so as to instill good behavior patterns and healthy routines for life, but we all know that it is not possible always to do that. But thinking ahead and teaching some of these things when you can or when the moment presents itself will help your child in the future. I haven't given up on toileting issues, but it's not the focus of my day anymore.

That being said, independence is a goal all parents have for their children. Yet we need to remember that each child is different and that some will need more supports and more of our direct help for many years. Others will leave the nest to live in group homes or residential facilities—or to live on their own. Others will continue to live at home because the parents are concerned for their adult child's safety out in the world. Others are at home because there are not enough living options in their community. Some will leave home to go to college. The point is that adulthood looks different for each person on the spectrum.

No matter what the functioning level of the child is, we strive for her to reach her full potential. It may look different for each child, but as the years roll by, you want to see your child learning the skills she will need to be as independent as possible in adulthood. Even if she continues to live at home with you for a long time, perhaps she can be in charge of doing the laundry and take on similar routine chores that in themselves can represent great strides forward.

This chapter is by no means a complete overview of the topic of self-sufficiency. Rather, it is a glimpse at certain areas that have presented challenges to some adults on the spectrum—areas that could perhaps have been improved, either slightly or greatly, if they had been addressed in childhood.

What Adults on the Spectrum
Have to Say About Independence

When talking about self-sufficiency, adults on the spectrum say the two areas that pose the greatest challenges are executive functioning (being able to get and stay organized) and sensory processing.

Dena Gassner believes that a big problem area for many on the spectrum is their lack of organizational skills. Some, like Michael Crouch, the postmaster, have innate organizational skills, but for most, it is an area of great need. This prevents some adults from taking advantage of possible employment opportunities. Dena believes that the teaching of organizational skills should be given the highest importance during the school years, along with social skills. She feels strongly that these two very important areas—crucial for success in adulthood—are not emphasized enough at school.

Because of fine motor and organizational challenges, Nick Dubin has issues with self-care in adulthood. His fine motor skills are so poor that he thinks he may have dyspraxia (the inability to perform particular purposive actions usually due to brain damage). Things like changing a lightbulb, which most adults consider a simple task, are very difficult for him. He cannot easily work with basic equipment like screwdrivers. Because of these challenges, he often has to rely on his father for help. However, he is able to drive a car with ease; this type of paradoxical, uneven skill set is not at all uncommon among people with Asperger's syndrome. Nick reports that, organizationally, he has problems related to central coherence, meaning that he has a hard time seeing the forest for the trees. This makes him concentrate on small details when, in fact, he should be paying attention to the big picture. This results in his overlooking things that need to be done. He has since learned that he does better when he focuses intensely on one task rather than spreading his attention around to ten or fifteen things. This challenge with multitasking is a problem when it comes to home care and household management, but also affects other areas of life. For example, when he was a student teacher, he had many demands placed on him at once, and he would become so preoccupied with one demand that he would forget about all the others. He often forgot to pick up the children from their special classes (like physical education, music, etc.) because he was so busy trying to remember to take a note to the secretary or make copies of something that the teacher wanted.

Shopping for food is a necessary activity that involves both sensory tolerance and organizational skills, and is one that can be practiced while children are young. Many young children tantrum in the stores and it may be due to sensory overload. In *Life and Love*, Zosia describes shopping as an autistic nightmare precisely because of the sensory bombardment, confusion about the social aspects of shopping, and executive functioning challenges. Some of the suggestions Zosia makes are ones that could be adapted to start early on with children on the spectrum. For example, to help with the organizational aspect of shopping, Zosia suggests making a map of the store layout. Some stores have these already. Then figure out which aisles the child's favorite items are on. Have the child make a list of needed/wanted items. These items can be organized by aisle. Map out the child's best shopping route before going into the store. Keep it brief, especially at the beginning, maybe shopping for just two or three motivating items that the child has chosen. Make a list, either written or with picture icons, that the child can see and you can read to him. If the child has sensory issues, this will help keep him focused. Sunglasses or a baseball cap and earphones or a Walkman can help if the child cannot be easily desensitized. Going at a time when there are fewer shoppers is also highly recommended.

Organizing and planning are necessary for everyone on the spectrum, at different levels. We usually tend to speak about these "executive functions" only when discussing people with Asperger's or the more functionally able, but everything we do in life takes planning and organizing, and should be taught to everyone. This is especially important when children get into junior high. For example, if your child has different subjects or classes at school, color code the textbook and the notebook that go together. Making a map of where the classrooms are and color coding to match the books the child has to take there are helpful.

Temple Grandin is a visual thinker and she organizes things in categories, in essence what Zosia is suggesting in terms of shopping. This is a helpful tip not only for home but also for special education classrooms, where color coding needed supplies by categories can help a child learn to organize what she needs to complete a task.

Planning, flexibility, and problem solving are not easy for most on the spectrum. It's a good idea to try and find some opportunities to practice these skills. A good way to do this is to take a skill a child already knows very well, and does unprompted, and then "sabotage" the situation. For example, if Mark knows how to set the table for four people, remove the forks from where he normally gets them (the drawer) and put them in the dishrack. Then when he sets the table and he sees the empty fork container, prompt him to look in the dishrack. Do that until he gets it, then change the situation around so sometimes the forks are in the drawer. Next, choose another item and start moving it around. Eventually he will understand that he needs to look for it. For verbally astute children, you can create social stories, again using situations for which they are very familiar with the rules. For example, you could take the rule, "If you fall and hurt yourself, go see the teacher," and change it by adding, "The teacher is out sick, who do you go see?" and so on. The point of these sabotage exercises is not to confuse children, but to help them gain flexibility and the notion of problem solving, so that when situations change in real life, they will be able to come up with a game plan.

Michael Crouch has never had problems with organizational skills. He reports always having been able to put things together and in order. Now as the postmaster general of the Crown College of the Bible, he has

PRACTICAL TIP

Think about where your child is at in terms of self-help and chore skill acquisition. What would a child her age typically be able to do, and what can your child do? Make a list of what your child can do, and what she can't. Do you see a pattern with the types of tasks she learns more easily and the ones she is having difficulty with? This will help you see the areas of difficulty you need to find strategies to help her with. As she gets older, the needed skills will change, and more will be added. Eventually, as an autistic adult going to live elsewhere, she will need to learn other household management skills. Starting good habits when young is useful for the long run.

336 student mailboxes to deliver mail to, along with the college offices' mail, all of which he first sorts alphabetically.

Despite his organizational strengths, Michael shares that he did a poor job of taking care of his body until he was an adult. He hardly ever brushed his teeth and bathed only once a week. When he first started shaving, he would cut his nose and ears. He was a bed wetter for years. When he went off to college, bed-wetting was the bad hygiene skill that got him into trouble. He was asked to wash his sheets every day, as well as to bathe. This got him into the routine of taking good care of himself, including brushing his teeth every day.

Sometimes adults on the spectrum can find others to help them with their sensory difficulties. In his book *Born on a Blue Day*, Daniel Tammet describes how, as a teenager, he hated having to shave. He used to cut himself, and it would take him an hour at a time and his skin would feel to raw and itchy afterward. So Daniel rarely shaved, but then the stubble would grow into a beard, which pulled on his skin. He couldn't stand the sensation, meaning he would have to shave. The bathroom would then be off limits to his siblings for hours while he shaved. Now, it is his partner who shaves him quickly once a week with an electric shaver, which he tolerates.

Temple Grandin talks about how it is really important to teach the skills

AUTISTIC ACHIEVEMENTS: THERE IS ALWAYS HOPE

Here's what bestselling author Donna Williams has to say on her blog (http://blog.donnawilliams.net) about how she became a qualified bath runner:

This morning I ran a bath. I then announced to my husband Chris that I could now run baths.

I'm 43.

I've been trying to run baths for 28 years.

I flood them, run them without the plug, run them cold, run them boiling, get in at the wrong time (ouch), forget them till they're stone cold. I'm sure this is familiar to all of you. But imagine this is 80–90% of every bath you ever ran. Its very hard to maintain confidence and keep trying. So this time I waited till I had ran 3 months of baths which actually worked! Then I was ready to say, yes, I can run a bath.

In childhood I got into the bath when made to. At about age 9 I was made to bathe with my infant brother. That taught me about having bodies (because I could see objectively he was a little person in the bath), about soap and washing but I couldn't work out that I had a whole body so I'd only rub some soap on one part or another. Then I learned my body was like a road map and ran the soap all along the lines. When I was about 11, I went to my cousins' house and they played in the bath and that taught me having a bath could actually be fun and you could even laugh in the bath (now there was a novel concept) and I got into shampoo (and drinking it), bubbles (filled the WHOLE room with these once . . . I think it was shampoo in the bath) and then got into the bath in my clothes, washed my clothes then took them off to wash the body underneath (made sense to me but I couldn't tell anyone what I was doing so it just seemed odd to them).

Then I realised the bath could be the one-stop-shop so I got in in my clothes, peed in them, washed the clothes, washed me then let the water out (yes, pretty gross but it was innovative and toilets do involve peeing then letting the water go so you might realise it was actually rather logical to use the bath in this inventive adapted manner but not really in keeping with the rules of the world—which I had no idea of and valued far more highly my individuality, autonomy and solitude). Then came my teens and I learned to use the shower. Lots of getting burned, lots of flooding, lots of leaving the shower running for hours after leaving it, lots of people yelling. I learned to associate baths and showers with people yelling and being called stupid. I kept trying.

I was assisted to leave my family's house (they had more challenges than me) in my teens at 15, and living alone was big time chaos as you can imagine. The details are in **Nobody Nowhere** and in fact my bath sagas are mentioned in many of my books, but regarding baths we are talking major flooding, weekly if not daily. We are talking soggy neighbors ceiling, we are talking water through the entire flat, we are talking lots of mess and shouting. I reverted to a wash cloth and a basin of water, it was safer. Then living with men (this was the version of care in the community for folks like me with few living skills and no professional or family support) meant I could get into their bath, their shower. So at least I'd mastered washing! But I so wanted to really 'get this.'

So I kept trying and I taught myself to get out of a boiling bath in my 30s and used a wall poster I made to sequence the running of a bath (when the plug goes in, the regulation of temperature, which order to put the body in).

But still the attention span and meaning blindness thing kept me flooding everything (forgot what the bath WAS or the noise).

So finally I started using a timer. But I kept walking off from the timer! I blocked the bathroom door so I couldn't leave . . . that worked for a while . . . like an imprisoned cat . . . I still forgot why I was there. I got a louder timer with an alarm. Then I progressed to carrying it with me via a rule that I was never allowed to leave a set timer without it coming with me. Finally, finally, FINALLY, I can run baths. I'm now going for one.

The moral is, even with half a brain, you can probably master something eventually if you keep trying new ways to counter the whole gamut of challenges which are obstacles to the activity.[9]

of good hygiene because people on the spectrum don't intrinsically grasp that this is important, and yet it is essential, particularly for those who are in contact with the real world every day. In my book *Adolescents on the Autism Spectrum*, I discussed the area of hygiene and grooming at length because of how important appearance is during those teen years. However, it is never too early to start teaching these skills. Some have trouble with hygiene because they don't have the motor skills; some don't get the social reason of *why* good hygiene is necessary. Others might have problems with sequencing. Many have sensory issues. For some it may be a combination of all of the above. One only has to read the excerpt from Donna Williams's blog (see "Food for Thought," pages 118 to 119) to see how many different parts of "taking a bath" can create problems for a person on the spectrum.

It is also a good idea to start teaching children at an early age so that they establish routines before they hit the turbulent teen years. Because of the wide variety of challenges and different ability levels, certain things come easily for some and are difficult for others; no one strategy is going to work for everyone. Before you can help a child, you need to do a task analysis and figure out which part of a routine is creating a challenge—and why—and then figure out how to teach it. How you teach that depends on why the child is having difficulties with a certain step. Some suggestions:

- For problems with sensory challenges: Use desensitization techniques or therapies that help with sensory processing.
- For problems with sequencing: Use a visual and or an auditory schedule (a taped recording).
- For problems with initiation and motor planning: Do hand-over-hand prompting and repeatedly "motor" a person through the physical aspect, then decrease the prompt.
- For all of the above: Use video modeling or music and songs to help the child learn and remember.

These same suggestions may be useful for teaching chores around the house, which gives children a sense of responsibility and introduces the concept of participating and contributing to the family unit. As the child gets older, volunteering can also be a way for him to give back to the community, which is a good idea because with all the people working so hard to help him, he needs to learn the concept of giving back.

Temple Grandin says that sometimes children have to be pushed a bit to get over some of their anxieties, in order to become more self-sufficient. For example, when Temple was a young girl, her mother wanted her to stay at her aunt's farm for the summer, and Temple was hesitant to go. Her mother said that she had to try it for two weeks, and if

PRACTICAL TIP

Explaining to your child or student *why* she needs to establish good self-care routines—the need for good hygiene to stay healthy and the social aspects of needing to smell good and look clean—is important. Some on the spectrum don't automatically understand why it is important to do certain things that are difficult for them. Using social stories can be helpful, and allowing them to choose their own hygiene products (cutting pictures out of magazines and newspapers and then shopping for them) can give them more ownership of their self-care.

she still wanted to come back, she would let her. Temple ended up having a great time, and staying on the farm gave her another opportunity to spend time with animals. When Temple got her driver's license, her mother made her drive to the store on her own. The key to pushing children on the spectrum is to know just how much you can push; you may create even more anxiety if you push too much.

As discussed in Chapter 1, Liane Holliday Willey, Brian King, and Jack Donehey-Nykiel have challenges with orientation mobility for different reasons. Liane has many challenges with sensory processing, and her visual processing affects her orientation mobility. She cannot rely on her own perception, especially under the duress of sensory overload. Brian remembers the difficulties in switching from elementary school to junior high because he had a tough time getting from room to room and so the first week of school he was late for every class. Jack also has challenges in the area of orientation mobility and used to get lost a lot before he learned how to ask for help.

Challenges in orientation mobility usually show up during the move from elementary school to junior high, because it is in junior high that students start having to change classrooms and teachers every hour or two. Liane, Brian, and Jack figured out some strategies to help them get around once they were in the situation, but now that we know that this is an area of difficulty for many, we can start teaching children while they are young how to get around in a new location. For example, we can take the child to a new school a few different times when it is empty and walk

LEARNING RESPONSIBILITY

Here's what Michael Crouch, college postmaster at the Crown College of the Bible, has to say about gaining responsibility as a child. He was diagnosed with PDD-NOS at age eleven.

The people who were the most influential on me were: my Mother (Ann Pustinger), my pastor (David Price), my youth director (Chris Hanks), and girls who were my age.

I learned responsibility by: (1) helping the coaches at my school, (2) having a baby brother to help raise, and (3) Mom giving us chores to do. With coaches, I helped set the field for PE and carried in/out equipment (I got credit for this and for dressing out). My school was known for having a good basketball team in our conference. The coach asked me to video the games for him (he would watch them and learn our mistakes and help verify the stats). I actually had to watch and put together: a VHS video camera, a tripod, case, a bag, 7-plugs-in-one, a camera lens, and an extension cord. I had no way of knowing that it would prepare me for today (I help video our church services live for our Internet broadcast, www.faithforthe-family.com)! At the end of 9th grade, I got a baby brother, Gregory! I had to adapt to having to help babysit almost every day. I did get in trouble for not doing some things at first (yes, like change diapers), but I learned to love him and enjoy having him around. I did spend my after-school hours having to watch him. I remember one year I got to stay home (not be counted absent) to watch him for 2 days! My senior year of high school I was "late" almost every day having to babysit until a babysitter came, but I did not get in trouble. Every thing I did, he did! Today Gregory is going into 9th grade and wants to follow me here to the Crown College!

■   ■   ■   ■   ■   ■   ■   ■   ■   ■   ■

around, videotaping the places with obvious landmarks and taking photos of those landmarks to remember. Then, going back to the school when it is crowded and going over the same areas is helpful. Also, if there are any maps available, highlighting the paths to take and explaining them to the child can be very useful.

Conclusion

Independence is a goal we all have for our children, but we may be parenting for longer than parents of neurotypical children. Thanks to the help of parents, teachers and other professionals, and peers, many adults on the spectrum report learning or improving skills even later in life. Challenges in executive functioning (such as organizing and planning) and sensory processing are often obstacles to self-sufficiency, but there are ways to make things easier. A few examples of techniques to try include color coding, making lists, categorizing, and mapping out unfamiliar areas. Doing chores helps teach all children responsibility—an essential foundation for self-sufficiency.

8

Social Relationships

TEACHER: Who do you go to when you have problems or need help at home, at school or in the community?
JEREMY: My mom, Allan. Mom loves me. Allan likes me. You understand.

TEACHER: What qualities do you possess that make you a good friend?
JEREMY: Exciting, strong listener, teacher of autism, I can offer experience of autism to people who are interested. Joker, kind, share outsider feeling.

TEACHER: What social/interpersonal needs do you have that are not being met at this time?
JEREMY: No friends at night.

—Allan Gustafson, interview with Jeremy Sicile-Kira, spring 2007

Relationships have always been difficult for Jeremy, especially when he was little. I tried to arrange play dates with other children, or enroll him in toddler groups in Paris and in the United Kingdom, where we lived. But he basically played on his own. Since he did not show much interest in the other children and he could not verbally communicate with them, it was hard for the children to sustain any kind of relationship once they were old enough to talk. Even when he learned turn-taking games and appropriate play, he was not interested in engaging in these activities outside a classroom or therapy setting, probably because of the sensory challenges that existed in those child-filled environments.

If you look at Jeremy's body language even now, through a neurotypical lens, it is not apparent that he wants to have friends and relationships. However, he does. When Jeremy was first introduced to the litewriter (which produces voice output for whatever words he spells), he was thrilled because this device was now giving him a "voice." Jeremy explained on MTV's *True Life*: "I Have Autism" that he wants to have friends, and having a voice by means of the litewriter made him feel that this was now possible. Although he communicated through the litewriter that he wanted to have a birthday party, once it was happening, he had to leave occasionally because he was overwhelmed by all the noise and attention.

During his senior year of high school, his friend Andriana would came over about twice a month to read books to him and discuss them with him. At the time, Jeremy was reading *The Adventures of Huckleberry Finn* for his high school English class. One day as Andriana was leaving, Jeremy spelled out, "May I haggle a hug out of you?" Another time, he saw a cousin who lives back east whom he hadn't seen in a while, and he asked her if she had a boyfriend. She said yes and that they had been dating for some time. Jeremy spelled out, "Are you angling to get married to him?" He is aware of social and romantic dynamics, and even wants to have those types of relationships in his own life, in his own time.

The Complexities of Social Relationships

It is a fallacy to think that children on the spectrum do not want to have friends or relationships. Those who can communicate make it clear they enjoy having friends and relationships, as do even those who are nonverbal such as Sue Rubin, Amanda Baggs, and DJ Savarese, whose comment to me was: "I have a few good friends. Very good friends say hopeful things and goldenly desire to hope fresh ideas are heard."

However, knowing you want to relate to other people is not the same as knowing *how* to relate, and this is difficult for all children on the autism spectrum, regardless of their functioning level. As for everything else, the difficulties may vary from child to child, but relationship skills need to be taught to all. Besides the challenges that most kids on the spectrum have with communication, they have problems recognizing faces, getting used to people's voices, and dealing with sudden movement. Then there are the sensory stimuli present in social environments that can be overwhelming for many, as has been discussed in previous chapters. Autistic individuals don't always know how to begin, sustain, or end a conversation, or understand the subtleties of body language. All this impacts relationship building in one way or another.

To complicate things further, there are different types of relationships, and each one has its own sets of social rules that become apparent over time to nonautistic children. However, they are not apparent to those on the spectrum. The child-parent relationship is different from the child-teacher relationship, and that is different from the child-peer relationship, and for each one, the social skills may be different. There are many other types of social interactions—with tutors, with respite workers, with neighbors, store clerks, and so on. As the child grows older and heads toward adulthood, there are dating relationships, sexual relationships, and for those needing twenty-four-hour support, there are relationships with caregivers and support persons. As the child grows older, he needs to learn the rules for all kinds of relationships—including the ones that now exist through the Internet, which has its own set of safety concerns that need to be addressed with those on the spectrum.

Often when it comes to autism skill building, we think about social skills, and of course these are important. But just as important are the skills of *interdependence*—that is, asking for help, telling people what your needs are, communicating with a store clerk, networking for possible job opportunities, and so on. Children on the spectrum do not tend to naturally ask for help, and these types of skills need to be taught and encouraged from an early age, as will be discussed later in this chapter. Nonverbal children need to be taught to do this with whatever alternative communication system works for them (see Chapter 2).

PRACTICAL TIP

As discussed in Chapter 2, finding a communication system that works for your child is very important. Once a system has been selected (whether it be a picture symbol system, a text-based communication device, or another method), it needs to be integrated into all the different social relationships. This takes some teaching and practice to generalize into other environments and relationships. Learning to express her wants, or ask for help in the classroom, at home, and then in a familiar store, restaurant, or library is a good way to start. Using the communication system in a social context such as in playing games or with a peer buddy at lunchtime can help create those social connections many nonverbal children are missing out on.

Teaching the Rules of Appropriate Social Behavior Should Begin Early

Many adults on the spectrum spoke to me about the need for learning rules of social behavior (i.e., social skills), and that this would have been extremely helpful as children. For children in general, it can be confusing to learn about all the different types of relationships, and for those on the spectrum, it is much harder. This will be an area of difficulty, no matter how functionally able or academically gifted—or not—a person on the spectrum is. Although not all children are verbal or have the communication skills that authors Temple Grandin, Stephen Shore, Michael John Carley, or Zosia Zaks do, *all* children can be taught about different relationships and appropriate behavior for each, and this is discussed later on in this chapter.

In his book, *Look Me in the Eye: My Life with Asperger's*, John Elder Robison describes the difficulties in trying to make friends when he was little. When he started nursery school, he attempted to make friends with one little girl by patting her on the head. His mother had shown him how to pet his poodle on the head to make friends with him, so he assumed the same would work with his classmates. When he saw playmates playing differently than he did with the trucks and blocks, he felt compelled to show them the right way—his way—of playing. Needless to say, none of these tactics went over well. John also shares that when he was nine, he had a life-changing revelation—he figured out how to talk to other children. Up until then, he would answer with whatever he was thinking when someone tried to initiate a conversation. For example, if someone said, "Look at my Tonka Truck," he might reply, "I rode a horse at the fair" or "I want some cookies," instead of "That's a neat truck. Can I hold it?"

It is obvious in reading *Unwritten Rules of Social Relationships: Decoding Social Mysteries Through the Unique Perspectives of Autism* that coauthors Temple Grandin and Sean Barron have different social perspectives. Temple's sense of happiness and connection to the world originates from a logical, analytical way of thinking; she resonates more with intellectual pursuits than emotional relatedness. Temple's sense of being is tied to what she does, not what she feels. Children who share this kind of social perspective are usually those who immerse themselves in projects and learning; facts and figures and patterns are what they truly enjoy. They relate to people who share the same interests. Sean's social perspective is different. His connection to the world right from the start was emotionally oriented. He tried to understand the world from a social-emotional connection and was deeply affected when he and the world were out of sync with each other. Children who share this kind of perspective are ones who long for friends and peers with whom they can be emotionally connected.

Although Temple and Sean have different social perspectives, they are clearly in agreement that parents, teachers, and other adults need to take responsibility while a child is young to firmly establish behavior patterns that will help her as she matures. Sean believes it is adults who create the environment that teach children personal responsibility for their actions. He believes this is best done by linking behavior with consequences and by teaching appropriate replacement behaviors.

Temple describes how much easier it was to understand appropriate rules of behavior when she was growing up in the 1950s. She points out that manners were more important back then and that everyone shared

PRACTICAL TIP

If your child or student likes visuals, draw a diagram of the hierarchy at school—principal, school secretary, school nurse, teacher, coach, instructional aide, students, crossing guard, and so on, and discuss the different ways the child might address these different categories of people. Also include whom the child might approach for different types of help. Having a list to refer to and practicing different scenarios can be helpful. This can be done with various communication systems, depending on the skill level of the child.

the same rules. For example, every mother in the neighborhood had the same expectations, so no matter whose house the neighborhood kids were playing at, the same rules of behavior applied. This is not so today. In my discussions with Temple, it became apparent that being taught good manners and rules of behavior was very important to her developing the notion of what was appropriate behavior in social situations. Temple says that children with autism need to be given clear rules as to what the expected behavior is and that, more important, consequences must be given when someone is not behaving in the expected manner. Temple believes that it is never too early to implement good, sound parenting strategies in the home and to establish expectations for appropriate behavior.

However, Temple also makes it clear that parents and teachers need to be able to tell the difference between bad behavior, which deserves a consequence, and behaviors that are due to sensory overload or some other autism-related challenge (as discussed in previous chapters). In those cases, it is appropriate intervention, not behavioral consequences, that will help the child.

In my discussions with her, Temple explained that she believes people with Asperger's who are now in their fifties and sixties generally had an easier time finding and keeping jobs because the social rules and expected behavior were clearer when they were growing up. She also shares how she almost lost her first job because she did not know that, as

DIFFERENT SOCIAL PERSPECTIVES

*Looking back, I'd have to say that I am a product of my environment. The
social structure of the 1950's and 60's was much simpler than it is today. Family
structure was strong, people exhibited a higher degree of respect towards each
other than they do today, and behavior expectations were more clearly defined.
Children were taught manners, consideration for others and to do good deeds in
the community. . . . Mother never viewed my autism as excusing me from the
expectation that I would function within the social structure. Even at age 6 I was
expected to eat dinner with the family, to behave properly and to respect the family
rules. . . . It was simply assumed, without question, that I would learn these social
skills.*

—Temple Grandin, page 3

*Even from a young age, I remember wanting desperately to have a revered place in
others' hearts, a desire largely incompatible with having heavy fear in my own
heart. This Catch-22 of social functioning caused a circular chain of events to
unfold as the years went by, starting as early as age five. . . . Allowing in only tiny
tidbits of information was the only way I knew to make sense of my environment. . . . The problem with going through my early years like this was I was missing experiences that I needed in order to develop the social skills I so desperately
wanted.*

—Sean Barron, pages 60, 62

Both quotes are from *Unwritten Rules of Social Relationships: Decoding Social
Mysteries Through the Unique Perspectives of Autism.*[10]

an employee, you can't talk to your boss in the same way as you would a
colleague. Temple would see what she considered mistakes at work, and
how the company could be run better, and often write letters to the boss
telling him how he could improve things. This was not appreciated, and
a mentor explained to her by drawing a diagram of the workplace hierar-

chy and the different type of conversation appropriate at each level that this was not how she should approach the boss.

Temple gave me an example of how her mother taught her good social behavior by using teachable moments. Temple's first trip to another city occurred when she was eight years old, traveling by train with her mother from Boston to New York. On the way home, a few Catholic nuns were sitting in the same railroad car. Temple had never seen nuns and was impressed by their "funny hats" and wanted to go talk to them. Her mother told her she could go talk to them, she could talk about New York and what she had seen, but she must not ask about the "funny hats" they were wearing. After ten minutes of discussion with the nuns, her mother called her back. It was a good experience all around, and a memorable one.

Temple told me about the time she was at an airport and met a young man with Asperger's and his mother. They went to a coffee shop and had something to drink. The young man saw a police officer sitting at another table and yelled over to him, "Is it your job to keep bad people in line?" Then, near the boarding gate, he saw two soldiers and yelled out, "Have you guys been to Iraq?" across the waiting room. Temple says that this sort of behavior can be avoided by giving children and teens specific instruction, for example to "approach the soldiers quietly, introduce yourself, say you are interested in the military, and then ask them, 'Have you ever been deployed?'" Teaching alternative appropriate social behaviors is much more effective than giving no instruction, waiting to see an inappropriate behavior, and then extinguishing it.

The Circles Program: Teaching the Unwritten
Rules of Social Relationships

The Circles Program, devised by Marilyn P. Champagne and Leslie W. Walker-Hirsch, is a useful tool for teaching children on the spectrum about social relationships. A scalable model that can be simple or complex, it provides a good foundation that can be built upon as time goes on. On a piece of poster board or large piece of paper, draw six concentric

---

PRACTICAL TIP

Using the visual of the Circles Program along with the notion of private and public discussed in Chapter 3 can help in teaching the unwritten rules of social relationships discussed earlier. Linking it all together will make the lesson easier to
learn. Even if the child is an auditory learner, the visual helps the parent or educator keep it all straight. Using social stories created with the child will reinforce
what is appropriate in certain relationships (i.e., the Private Circle) and what is
not in other types of relationships, as outlined in the Circles Program.

---

rings, as you would see in a tree trunk. Each circle represents different
levels of relationships, from the inner circle, which is the Private Circle,
to the outer circle, which is the Stranger Circle.

The different levels to teach are:

Private Circle—Mom, dad, siblings
Close Hug Circle—Relatives
Far-Away Hug Circle—Good friends
Handshake Circle—People you know that you are friendly with,
   some classmates
Wave Circle—Neighbors, mailman, other classmates
Stranger Circle—People you don't know

This model can be personalized for each child. Photos that represent
each person can be put into their respective circles. Over time, this poster
will change, with people moving from one circle to another and new
people being introduced. For example, when a child is very young, her
teacher may be in the Far-Away Hug Circle (she may give a hug at arm's
length as opposed to a close hug, which involves more physical contact),
but as the child gets older, the teacher should be moved to the Handshake Circle. This is because when a child gets older, she needs to learn
that it is socially inappropriate to hug every grown-up she meets or
knows. For children who are communicating, the different types of con-

> ## PRACTICAL TIP
>
> To teach the unwritten rules of social relationships, think of the "hidden curriculum," mentioned in previous chapters. If you realize your child appears clueless in terms of certain social situations (such as asking strangers personal questions, not knowing how to sustain a conversation instead of a monologue, or approaching a potential playmate as he would his pet dog), make a note of it. Then, write down what the rule is for that social behavior and explain it to the child. Write a social story with the child using the rule, then practice. Have the child engage in role playing with a sibling or other willing person who enjoys acting. Reminding him of the rule when necessary will help him to remember. Keeping the rules and social stories in a binder for easy reference and review can be helpful as well.

versation that are appropriate for each type of relationship can be explained here. For example, telling people in the Private Circle about how you feel is okay, but talking to people in the Stranger Circle is not. Over time, the kinds of conversation change as well. For a teenage girl to announce at the breakfast table to her family (Private) that she has just gotten her period is okay, but it is *not* appropriate to announce it in the school cafeteria at lunchtime (Handshake and Wave Circles).

Care must be taken to explain certain unwritten rules of social relationships, such as the fact that just because someone acts *friendly* doesn't mean he is a *friend*. These are the kinds of things that children on the spectrum need to be taught.

Acting Classes: A Good Place to Learn and Master Social Behavior

Many teens on the spectrum have reported that acting classes and drama clubs have been a great way for them to develop social confidence. Elijah Wapner, the comedian from MTV's *True Life*: "I Have Autism," says that the best social skills program for him has been performing comedy and developing himself as an actor. Elijah started getting up on stage when he was thirteen years old. Since then he feels much more confident socially. When an individual learns acting and performance, he starts with a script, which is always a safe way to be in a new setting. Then, as the actor learns his lines, he also learns what facial expressions and gestures are appropriate to the situation and how to give expressiveness to his voice. Not every child will be able to get up on stage and entertain an audience, but acting-for-nonactors classes and other such lessons can provide a safe environment for basic skill and confidence building.

The Need to Teach Interdependence

When I discussed the subject of independence with autism consultant Dena Gassner, who is herself on the spectrum, she pointed out that the main challenge faced by many on the spectrum (at least those on the functionally more able end) is not independence, but *interdependence.*

I had never thought of it that way, but Dena's comment was echoed by many other adults on the spectrum whom I have interviewed. They remember growing up as children very independent by nature of their lack of social skills, but were unable to ask for help or approach people in an appropriate manner to make a connection. Since people on the spectrum have difficulties with communication and all that is social, they tend not to have problems with the notion of being alone or independent (although many need supports for everyday tasks). In America, we encourage people to volunteer and help others, but we also value and reward independence and the ideal of the "self-made man." Yet we live in a society that in reality functions only if we are interconnected and willing to exchange services, network, help other people, and ask for help. As adults, people get jobs or clients through networking— telling others they are looking for work, asking for referrals, and so forth. Adults on the spectrum don't usually do this naturally. This goes beyond the usual social skills training provided to children on the spectrum.

Zosia Zaks in *Life and Love* talks about the need to teach autistic people certain rules about approaching another person in social situations they are unsure of, including whom to approach, when and how to do it, and what to tell the other person. For example, when and how do you tell someone that something bad has happened, or whom do you tell when someone asks you to do something that you do not think is appropriate?

Many of the adults on the spectrum whom I spoke to told me that it took them a very long time to realize that to be interdependent was okay, that most of us nonautistics survive and thrive because we know how to be interdependent and how to give and take assistance and make connections, something people on the spectrum don't just learn by osmosis. We should strive to have our children be as independent as possible in certain areas of their lives. However, the interdependence piece is a skill that truly needs to be mastered by all and should be taught from early on.

Children who require one-on-one-aide support need to learn to ask when they need help instead of just being "taken care of." They also need to learn how to relate to others without the layers of support. If a person still requires supports as a teen or an adult, he will need to learn more about requesting assistance and giving his direction on how he needs that help.

Those children who have no aide supports also need to develop skills in this area, in order to be prepared for various aspects of adulthood, from "networking" for jobs and finding a place to live, to applying for and doing well in college if that is on the horizon.

As mentioned in Chapter 3, safety supports are necessary, too, such as having a Safe Activities List. Zosia Zaks believes that having a buddy system in place is another important support to children in the social arena. Zosia suggests that one or two trusted children that the child is comfortable with be identified as buddies whom the child can call on when in doubt about the safety of a certain social situation—for instance, if someone asks the child to leave the playground, to get in a car, and so forth.

Social Rules Are Important Guideposts for Interdependence

Temple Grandin remembers that her area of particular difficulty was not doing things independently, but having to deal with the social inter-

FOOD FOR THOUGHT

THE HIDDEN CURRICULUM—HELPFUL RULES THAT NEED TO BE TAUGHT

As long as things followed the set of rules I could play along. Rules were—and are—great friends of mine. I like rules. They set the record straight and keep it that way. You know where you stand with rules and you know how to act with rules. Trouble is, rules change, and if they do not, people break them. I get terribly annoyed when either happens. Certain things in life are givens. "Thank you" is followed by "You are welcome." You hold doors open for other people. The elderly are treated with respect. You do not cut in front of other people, you stay in line and wait your turn. You do not talk loud in libraries. Eye contact is made when you talk to someone. The list goes on, but the intent never changes: rules are maps that lead us to know how to behave and what to expect. When they are broken, the whole world turns upside down.

—Liane Holliday Willey, *Pretending to Be Normal: Living with Asperger's Syndrome*[11]

action when she needed assistance. For example, when she first learned to drive, she was not nervous about driving to the store by herself, but she was anxious about interacting with the clerk in the store. When she had to stay at a hotel for the first time by herself, she was not nervous about staying alone in a strange place; rather, she was nervous about having to go through the check-in process with the receptionist. The first time she had to put gas in the car, she was anxious about having to ask the gas attendant for help.

For children on the more functionally able end of the spectrum, the social aspects of a situation may present them with the most difficulty, but because they appear so able at the physical aspects of any task such as shopping or visiting the library, we often forget that they still need to be taught the social piece. For those more impacted by autism, we often focus on the functional aspects of a skill (and rightly so) and the social aspect is really another step to teach.

Starting when children are young to instill the idea of interdepend-

---

PRACTICAL TIP

Social stories and practice are good ways for children to learn from whom and how they should ask for assistance and in what situations (such as the situations Temple Grandin describes, as well as needed interaction with store clerks, waiters, security guards, and librarians). Making simple videos of situations using friends or family and others unfamiliar to your child or student for the child to watch can be helpful. Then play-acting the same circumstance can reinforce the lesson. For some, working on one social situation can be helpful. For example, to teach about shopping and the necessary skills of asking which aisle a certain item is in, finding it, and paying for the item, it is more effective to take a child to ten different stores one after the other for the same item on the same day than to buy many items in one store twice a week. Practice, practice, and more practice is necessary for some children.

---

ence and the ability to ask for assistance, or feel comfortable in these types of social relationships, will make it much easier for them when they are adults and have many other types of social needs.

The Importance of Having Autistic Peers and Nonautistic Peers

In Chapter 4, "Self-Esteem," I described how authors Amanda Baggs and Kamran Nazeer shared that having relationships with people with autism as well as nonautistic friends was important to building self-esteem.

Amanda says that being exposed to a variety of autistic people is crucial because there are autistic people she communicates easily with, and autistic people whose communication is totally alien and overloading to her even if they technically speak the same language. Amanda says conversations with nonautistic people are fraught with extremes of misinterpretation in both directions.

Author Stephen Shore also shared that there appears to be an increased

---

PRACTICAL TIP

If your child or student shows an interest or talent in a certain area, getting him involved with a small club or finding a knowledgeable mentor not only can help in learning more about the area of interest, but can also get him practicing his social skills and learning how to connect and have conversations with other people. Most towns and cities have different types of organizations based on different interests or hobbies—such as the San Diego Model Railroad Museum—and it is well worth the effort of searching them out.

---

rate of long-term relationships established between people on the spectrum and people who differ from them in some way—be it age, country of origin, or a cognitive difference. This is true of all kinds of relationships, whether it is marriage, close friendships, or other interactions.

Stephen's advice to parents is that unless the relationship is clearly harmful, the relationships their children choose (e.g., with an older age group or with foreigners) should be encouraged so that they can have the friends they want.

Relationships can also develop over special interests. Temple Grandin often talks about how her social relationships have developed based on her interests. Her passion for animals and her interest in autism have provided her a way to connect to others. Exchanging ideas and information and sharing her knowledge have led to Temple's developing social relationships with many different types of people. This can be true for children and teenagers as well. Jason "J-Mac" McElwain, the autistic basketball player who scored 20 points in about four minutes in February 2006, loved the game and developed rapport with the basketball players at his school because of this love. Focusing on the shared interest and not the interaction takes away some of the anxiety that many feel when in a social situation.

Jack Donehey-Nykiel, the young man pursuing Islamic Studies, shared that relationships with his school-age peers were difficult as they were intrigued by Jack's knowledge on a variety of unusual subjects yet

FOOD FOR THOUGHT

THE IMPORTANCE OF ACCEPTANCE AND ENCOURAGEMENT
IN DEVELOPING SOCIAL RELATIONSHIPS

When he was a teen, Michael Crouch was fortunate to have a wonderful peer group that also helped him transition to college life.

For communication and relationships, I do have to thank the girls! I did have trouble with public speaking, speaking too fast/too low, eye contact, and stuttering. Yes, I was known for my temper tantrums when I did not get my way, or there was a sudden change in my routine. I did not have a voice you would want to listen to. When I was a teenager, at church we started a teen choir to sing once a week. I did not want to get in it. I knew I had no voice and I was scared to get in front of people. I had 5 girls in particular who spent every week for 2 years encouraging me to sing in the teen choir. They were persistent. They said I would like it. They did not put me down and remind me of my faults! I hated telling them no every week, but they did not give up. When I finally gave in, and joined the teen choir, they cheered as if I scored the winning point at the buzzer! A year later, the youth director decided I should sing with him in church (he could not sing), but he told me after it was scheduled! I was scared to death, but 1 of the 5 girls told me that day "that I was going to go up there and do a good job no matter what anyone says or does!" I knew she was sincere. The youth group also had teen visitation (where the teens go invite people to church)—girls encouraged me to come! When I said I was coming to the Crown College, some of those girls were already here and they told me they were happy for me and encouraged me to get in the college choir. I quickly remembered learning my lesson with teen choir, and said I am in! My first year here in speech class the teacher gave out 5 sheets of vocal exercises and said if we would do these for 5 minutes every day it will help our voices. I did that (yawning to tongue twisters) for 5 minutes every day along with learning to use my lips and breathe at the belt buckle in college choir. Today I do have a nice voice that people like to hear whether it's "Blue Christmas" at Christmas parties, voicemails, and ripping the boys to ask the girls for the Valentine Banquet! I do not mind that today most of the people I see and work with are women.

confused at his lack of comprehension of the "hidden curriculum," and so he was at times bullied. More supportive teachers encouraged Jack to ignore the students who were attacking him and making fun of his interests. Since his junior year in high school, he has had a good friend with whom he shares common interests. This friend was introduced to him through one of his understanding teachers, and the relationship has been a wonderfully positive one.

Michael Crouch says that he learned to enjoy life by being around nonautistic girls and teenagers. His first friend in life was a girl who enjoyed singing and playing games. Despite the fact that Michael was the class nerd with a temper, this girl liked Michael and invited him to play with her at recess. She looked beyond his faults and saw his need for friendship. Similarly, it was teenage girls at church who encouraged him to become a member of the teen choir. Michael felt he had no talent in this area, but a group of girls every week for two years asked him to join the choir, and finally he did. These are the types of relationships that help our children grow in confidence, social skills, and fulfillment.

The Boys and Girls Clubs that offer after-school programs can be good places to foster relationships, although children on the spectrum need some peer training (and staff coaching as well) to ensure that this is successful. Finding a few children who are willing to develop a friendship or a circle of support is necessary or the child on the spectrum may get lost in the shuffle and find the environment overwhelming. As mentioned earlier, there are Best Buddy Clubs in the middle schools and high schools that can help foster these kinds of relationships. Also, many schools at all age levels have peer buddies that help the students in physical education classes. Both of these are good ways to find students willing to promote relationships with children on the spectrum. In the younger grades, many girls love to help out and can become natural mentors to their fellow classmates.

Relationships Can Get Easier in Adulthood

Stephen Shore says that peer relationships were difficult for him most of the time—until more recently. As a child, he found it difficult to relate

FOOD FOR THOUGHT

SENSORY OVERLOAD AFFECTS SOCIALIZING

Brian King, LCSW, explains on his informative website, www.ImAnAspie.com, why social gatherings can be difficult:

I prefer spending quiet time alone or with no more than a few other people. The more people, the more noise and movement therefore the more overloaded and anxious I get. My hearing is such that when more than one sound or voice is occurring simultaneously the sounds are processed in my brain into one noise. Therefore unless I really concentrate I can't decipher what's being said by someone I'm talking to if there are other sounds in the room. It's for this reason among others that I avoid social gatherings where many people will be in attendance.[12]

to grade school peers, and his friends tended to be older. Discussions Stephen has had with other adults on the spectrum indicate that relating more easily to older people than to peers is a common experience. This may be because those on the spectrum who have special interests or academic inclination find adults more open to discussing these topics than other children or teens. In fact, most teens consider studious peers to be nerds and that is not considered a positive trait in the middle school or high school environment, whereas adults are impressed by academic excellence and the passionate pursuit of knowledge.

Brian King, a clinical social worker and autism consultant, remembers that, as a child growing up, he was considered a social outcast at school. He describes his grade school experience as excruciating and states that his classmates made a point of making him feel different, as if that were a bad thing. Now, Brian says he has met some of those neurotypical peers who have finally matured into adults with an avid interest or career to pursue, and connecting to them is easier now that they are older and wiser. As well, adults tend to be less judgmental and more accepting of nerdiness than adolescents are. As adults, it is no longer about being cool, but about being successful, which usually entails having an area of expertise.

Brian says he now has a few wonderful people in his life, and these friends allow him to exhibit all of his Aspie eccentricities; he feels they even *appreciate* his quirks. He believes that there is no greater show of love and respect than to allow someone to be himself. However, one of the most heartbreaking experiences for Brian is when he reveals his Asperger's to others who have become so used to him acting in a neurotypical way that they insist he continue to do so. These people, while perhaps well meaning, don't understand that it is very tiring for him to continue to maintain eye contact, engage in chitchat, and be in environments that are overloading his senses—and more important, they are not able to accept him as he is.

Conclusion

Social relationships are difficult for everyone on the spectrum. It is a myth that children on the spectrum are not interested in having friends; many are, they just don't know how. There are different types of relationships—with parents, peers, teachers, friends, service people, and the like. The Internet has created an arena to provide friendships and support to people who have a hard time leaving home. Using a method like the Circles Program can help teach the different levels of relationships, and appropriate behavior and conversations based on each relationship. Acting classes can help teach body language and facial expressions and facilitate the learning of social skills. Children need to be taught interdependence skills—how to ask for help, how to approach a store clerk, and so on. Both autistic and nonautistic peers are important to developing social relationship skills—and both types of relationships should be encouraged.

9

Self-Advocacy

Jeremy recognizes that he does have a disability. He knows he has autism. He can clearly state his preferences and knows about himself, strengths and weaknesses. Jeremy has stated that his preferred method of instruction is auditory. He prefers working alone. When asked, "What is a disability?" Jeremy states, "People don't understand." Upon further questioning, it is *other* people, not the people with the disability. When asked if he understands what accommodations are, he states "changes." When asked if he has any accommodations in his class, he further spells, "Yes, but not enough. So much of the time is spent on group projects." Jeremy would prefer to spend more time in GE (general education) class, Sociology, but there is so much group time. Jeremy likes when the class has lecture and he can listen. It is evident in observational data by the time spent in class. On the days when it is lecture, Jeremy can spend 45–60 minutes in class, but when the class forms groups, Jeremy wants to leave class.

TEACHER: *What are your successful classes?*
JEREMY: *English, History, Sociology. I had very good teachers.*
  I learned a lot from them.

TEACHER: *What kind of support/help would assist you in being more successful in your classes?*

JEREMY: *Teachers understand my problem. Have people helping me with my work.*

TEACHER: *Are there any classes or activities you would like to take to help you reach your goal?*

JEREMY: *I like learning computers. Write books like mom.*

—Allan Gustafson, interview with Jeremy Sicile-Kira,
spring 2007

When he was a baby and young toddler, it was hard to know what Jeremy wanted. He never pointed or grabbed food choices put in front of him. Over time he learned to make choices and show us his preferences, finally practicing the most basic form of self-advocacy. As Jeremy got older, we gave him more control over putting his after-school schedule together. Then when he started junior high, we tried to prepare him for giving more input to his IEP (Individualized Education Program) meetings, which laid out what he would be taught over the year, but it was hard because his communication skills were very basic and we were not sure how much he understood since his expressive skills were so poor.

During high school he learned to communicate effectively and give input to the IEP process and planning his future. His teacher, Allan Gustafson, spent a lot of time teaching Jeremy to think about his strengths, how having autism impacted his life, and how he could use his strengths to help with some of the challenges. Allan taught him to use his newly found communication skills to talk about his feelings and his needs, and not to just react to the environment. This also meant that Jeremy had to take more responsibility for his actions. Allan spent a lot of time discussing the future with Jeremy, trying to find out what Jeremy wanted his life to look like down the road a bit and what he needed to learn and accomplish in order to get there.

A few months into his new transition program, Jeremy started acting out at home and at school, was unable to sleep at night, and was not his usual cheerful self. After a few weeks of this behavior, he communicated to me that he was sad and wanted to see his therapist. Jeremy shared with her that he was upset about a conversation he overheard between a long-term substitute teacher and Jeremy's instructional aide. His therapist suggested that Jeremy write a letter to the teacher. This is what he wrote:

To Teacher,

I have to say I heard you talk to my aide. I think you are wrong to tell her not to teach me academics. You know I want to go to college. I want to write a book about my life and people who have helped me, but also about people like you that give professionals a bad name. Good teachers like Allan and Maureen and Janine have helped me and not hindered me.

Also, academic goals and objectives are written in my IEP decided by a group of professionals. I get discouraged when professionals like you seemingly knowledgeable are not encouraging staff to teach what is in the IEP.

Sincerely,
Jeremy Sicile-Kira

It saddened and angered me to realize that after all of Allan's hard work and the careful IEP planning, Jeremy was being subjected to this type of negative and hurtful treatment. However, Jeremy's therapist was right-on in suggesting he write to the offending new teacher. How much more powerful than to have Mom write a letter! This whole situation was no fun, but in the end it made him a stronger person. For him to realize that he could advocate for himself, that he didn't need me to defend him or talk for him, was very empowering and a boost to his self-esteem. It validated what Allan and I have been trying to teach him over the last few years: that although he is nonverbal and severely impacted by autism, he can still have a voice and stand up for himself, and people will listen. He is becoming his own person.

The Importance of Teaching Advocacy Skills

While our children are growing up, whether they are fully included in general education classes or whether they spend most of their time in special education classrooms, they spend a lot of time learning to conform. They learn to sit and listen; they learn to say yes, to follow instructions, and to do what the teacher wants them to do. At home, they are also learning to conform to what other people are requesting them to do. Granted, some learn better than others, some have a difficult time with the concept of following rules, but most eventually get the picture. As these children grow older, we need to teach them to say no at appropriate times, to make choices, and to accept responsibility for their choices. As they mature into teens and head toward adulthood, they need to learn to think for themselves and not just do as they are told.

Giving choices, within parameters, to a young child on the spectrum, and respecting her choices, is a good way to start teaching self-advocacy. Children first rely on their parents, and little by little they learn to order in a restaurant, then to tell a shopkeeper what they are looking for, ask a teacher for help, or stick up for themselves when they are being picked on by classmates. Even those severely impacted by autism need to be able to make their wants and needs known. Making even basic, everyday choices is a starting point for self-advocacy.

Children who are fully included in general education programs have an even greater need early on to be aware of the sensory challenges they face and why, so that they can learn to ask for accommodations instead of having meltdowns caused by sensory issues when the teacher may have no clue as to what is going on. For this to happen, a child has to have a sufficient amount of self-awareness and a mentor whom she can model and who will work with her to help her reach a point where she can advocate for herself.

School is a good place to start learning how to advocate. School is a micro-society and a safe place to learn important life skills that can then be transferred to the community at large. In addition, in the United States, by the time a child is sixteen years old, he is expected to provide input to his IEP. The amount of input and what it looks like will vary depending on his

---

PRACTICAL TIP

No matter where a child is on the spectrum, self-advocating and understanding that he has the right to disagree with those in power are important safety skills. Although some children are aggressive, most tend to follow what they are asked to do, and this is not always a good thing. People who have power over our children (i.e., aides, camp counselors, therapists, other adults, etc.) do not always have the best intentions, although most do. Learning to say no is another form of self-advocacy and is an important skill especially in those teen years when peers may be enticing them to make poor choices. Using social stories of situations where a child or student should voice a different opinion or say no, and practicing these scenarios, is important.

---

functional ability level, but it still needs to take place. For those who are on the academic track, when they reach the age of eighteen and consider employment or college, they will have to be able to handle an interview by themselves and be able to ask for any accommodations they may need. Again, this is a skill those on the spectrum will not learn by osmosis.

Disclosure and Self-Awareness

The issue of disclosure is a heated one with parents, teachers, and adults on the spectrum. "Should we or should we not disclose, to whom and how?" is one of the questions I get asked most at my presentations (the topic of sex is still in first place, even at autism conferences). Often I meet parents of children with Asperger's syndrome who do not want to use the "A" word around their child, they do not want to tell the child about his diagnosis, or they do not want his classmates to know. As mentioned in Chapter 4, "Self-Esteem," people who were diagnosed as adults described feeling relieved because they had always known they were different, but didn't know why. Knowing *why* they were different empowered them. Now, having this label, they know where to look to access strategies to help in the areas they have challenges. As well, they are able to meet

**DISCLOSURE, SELF-AWARENESS, AND SELF-ADVOCACY:
WHAT ADULTS ON THE SPECTRUM HAVE TO SAY**

More and more people on the spectrum are learning to advocate for themselves. For those who have access to a computer, the Internet has opened up a whole new world of possibilities. Amanda Baggs, a mute autistic disability rights activist, has remarked that people like her may be isolated by sensory difficulties, but they can still communicate to many others from their own living room. On the Internet, a person can access resources that can help her, and she can communicate and blog with others on the spectrum. They can share information, advocacy, and advice, and they can support each other. Internet blogging has helped to create virtual online communities of support and discussion.

other adults on the spectrum and share resources, both online and offline.

There is general consensus among adults on the spectrum that the child should be told, because the child "feels" he is different anyway. To give a name to what he is feeling will help him feel better about himself. It is important that the child be told, but to be told in a positive matter, highlighting the strengths the child has that will help him overcome any areas of difficulty.

When it comes to telling others, opinions vary, although everyone tends to agree that self-advocacy and disclosure are linked. Some parents or adults with Asperger's syndrome may not wish to disclose the diagnosis of AS, but rather disclose how it affects them or a need they have, for example, "My eyes are sensitive to bright lights. Is it okay if I wear sunglasses to class?"

Some parents feel that their child may get to the point where he will be self-sufficient or neurotypical, and they don't want him to have a label. It is true that as a child gets older and becomes an adult, he "owns" the diagnosis and it should be his to share or not. However, if the fact that a child has Asperger's is not disclosed to school peers, they have no way of understanding why he acts or thinks differently, and this does not allow the opportunity for other classmates to help him.

FOOD FOR THOUGHT

THE LINK BETWEEN DISCLOSURE AND ADVOCACY

Self-advocacy and disclosure are inexorably linked because the need for self-advocacy begins when a person's needs are not being met in a given situation. Part of self-advocacy involves educating others of one's needs, and that usually includes reasons why; hence disclosure. The challenge is to accomplish this self-advocacy and disclosure in a way that promotes better mutual understanding, and therefore benefits all involved. For example after telling my wife why the ticking of an alarm clock was so troubling, she was able to have much greater empathy for my situation and remove the offending device.

Having a vehicle for developing self-advocacy and appropriate disclosure while in public school will pay great dividends in self-awareness and interfacing with the world as a "different" person later on.

—Stephen Shore, *Ask and Tell: Self-Advocacy and Disclosure for People on the Autism Spectrum*[13]

Zosia Zaks believes that parents should tell their children. Diagnosis is crucial to finding the help you need. If Zosia had known sooner why she had all her difficulties, she and her parents would have known where to look for strategies to help her. Knowing what your particular challenge is, she says, is constructive.

Dena Gassner, MSW, says that from her experience working with adults who are on the spectrum, the ones who are most successful as adults knew from the beginning that they were different. Giving a name to that feeling of difference, she believes, empowers the child. Teaching a child to be assertive is a good way to start teaching safety skills, as discussed earlier, but it is also teaching her to advocate for herself. For example, ordering food in a restaurant and teaching the child to clarify and be specific about what she wants is a good way to practice the skill of

PRACTICAL TIP

Parents of children who are on the more functionally able end of the spectrum have different opinions about whether or not to disclose their child's diagnosis to others. For some, it is not an easy decision to make. Making a list of the pros and cons of disclosure can be helpful. Think about your child's challenges and how she would be helped by having people around her know why she has them. If other people are not aware the child is on the spectrum, will they be understanding and appropriate about any differences or difficulties?

thinking about what it is you need and want, and learning to ask for it in an assertive but pleasant manner.

Nick Dubin feels strongly about disclosing his diagnosis. When asked, he says he cannot overemphasize the important of self-advocacy. Nick was diagnosed at age twenty-seven, and he can think of many employment situations when having had the diagnosis sooner and sharing it with his employers would have been beneficial. For example, Nick wanted to be a special education teacher. During his student teaching assignment prior to his diagnosis, the cooperating teacher assumed things about Nick that were not true. His inability to multitask was viewed as a lack of effort on his part, and some of his inappropriate behaviors were viewed as purposeful. For example, once he unthinkingly showed up at school wearing a sweatshirt from a jazz club on which there was a picture of a tequila glass. He was immediately reprimanded and told to go home and change his shirt.

Since receiving his diagnosis, Nick has tried to be an advocate for himself whenever possible. Upon entering the doctoral program in psychology where he is currently enrolled, he knew that he did not want to be a psychotherapist. Nick's problems with central coherence (seeing the big picture) would have made it almost impossible for him to effectively help clients with their issues. However, he did have a passion for teaching. In entering the doctoral program, he disclosed his Asperger's and explained that he could not be in the program if he was required to do a

2,000-hour psychotherapy internship. Nick explained that because of his Asperger's syndrome, he had a different set of skills that he thought could be useful and wanted to see if those skills could be pursued within the context of the school. Nick was pleasantly surprised when he was given the option to have alternate internships that would be more aligned with his personal career goals. So far, his disclosure has worked out for the better, although others on the spectrum have had different experiences.

Ruth Elaine Joyner Hane points out that there are different levels of disclosure and some gray areas. In *Ask and Tell: Self-Advocacy and Disclosure for People on the Autism Spectrum*, she gives the example of Betty, the checkout clerk at the local supermarket she frequents. She sees her often at the store but she is not a personal friend. When Ruth can't hear her because of her problems deciphering sounds in a noisy environment, she says, "Sorry, I have trouble hearing in a noisy area." She does not disclose her autism in such situations. Ruth prefers to disclose, little by little, information about herself, as needed. Furthermore, Ruth explains that self-awareness is a necessary precursor to self-advocacy. Understanding what emotional state you are in, and why you are feeling that way, will help you analyze what your needs are to then be able to ensure they are met, speaking up on an as-needed basis.

Liane Holliday Willey differs from Ruth when it comes to disclosure. In *Ask and Tell*, Liane describes herself as a "too-much-information" kind of person. She will tell people whom she doesn't know that she has Asperger's, sometimes even when it isn't necessary to state. Despite this difference, Liane agrees with Ruth that self-awareness, knowing who you really are and what you need, is essential for being able to advocate for yourself.

Advocacy Skills Are Teachable

Even young children can learn to self-advocate. In *Ask and Tell*, Kassiane Alexandra Sibley writes about teaching self-advocacy skills to those on the spectrum, and believes that it is best to start when they are young children, using a mentor or facilitator to help. The first step is planning and modeling. Kassiane gives the example of two first graders in different schools who are both light sensitive. In the first case, the boy is squinting because of the glare but the teacher thinks it is because he is having a hard time seeing, so she places him right in the front under the lights, where the glare from the whiteboard is even brighter. The boy is extremely uncomfortable but does not know what to do, so he continually turns the lights off or leaves his seat for a dark corner of the room. When he is reprimanded or punished for doing so, he has meltdowns.

The other first grader has a mentor, a college student who has Asperger's and who is a family friend. When the young girl tells the college student about her problem, they brainstorm and come up with ideas to propose to the teacher: take down the chalkboard, change the lighting system, give the student a different seat, ask if she can wear sunglasses and/or a hat. The mentor explains about giving the teacher options and what is reasonable and what is not (for example, removing the chalkboard or turning off the lights is not) and about the concept of compromise. The girl and her mentor go to see the teacher after school, the mentor introduces herself, says she has heard such good things about her (which is true), and then explains the light sensitivity issue and offers the possible solutions of changing seats and wearing a hat and sunglasses. The teacher agrees on changing the seat and the wearing of sunglasses. The following week the student and mentor meet, and the mentor asks if the accommodations are helping. The little girl says yes. This example shows how early on we can start children thinking about possible solutions to problems and how to discuss these rationally with another person, especially one in a position of power.

Kassiane believes that carrying cards or letters around explaining the person's autism and how it affects him is a good because even those who are verbal can become nonverbal in stressful situations. Similarly, it can be useful to carry a card with food allergies listed in order to communicate with restaurant staff to ensure that the ordered food fits in with the dietary needs; a card with emergency contact phone numbers is also a good idea.

In *Ask and Tell*, Stephen Shore says that there is no hard-and-fast answer as to when to begin teaching the concepts of self-advocacy and disclosure. However, he feels that a good time to start is when parents first learn that their child has a condition and needs special education services. Working with a young child will inspire notions of self-

FOOD FOR THOUGHT

SELF-SUFFICIENCY

Kassiane Alexandra Sibley is an independent young adult who has Asperger's syndrome. Like many her age, she was improperly diagnosed before discovering at age eighteen that she had an autism spectrum disorder. These excerpts are from "Help Me Help Myself: Teaching and Learning Self-Advocacy," a chapter she wrote in *Ask and Tell*, edited by Stephen Shore.[14]

Self-advocacy is a topic I find very extremely important because it is so rarely thought about and discussed. I have had to learn self-advocacy skills the hard way, and I do not want that for my younger peers. I find myself frustrated by parents and professionals who prefer to strive for "indistinguishable from peers" rather than self-sufficiency. Independence does not and should not have to equal typicality, but in so many people's eyes, the two are synonymous. I firmly believe that everyone on the Autism Spectrum can and should learn advocacy skills. . . .

The gift of advocacy is the most important gift we can give to ourselves and the next generation. Some day there will not be anyone around to help get our needs met. We are experts about our own needs and are, therefore, the ones who should be explaining our issues and ways to work around them. A well-meaning neurotypical person may know autism as a whole, but will not know autism as it applies to the individual in question.

determination and encourage him to focus on preferences and things he is good at, which will help him choose hobbies, courses, and then a career based on his interests. Stephen outlines how, with the help of a mentor, the IEP process can help a student over some years learn advocacy skills. Children can have more and more input as the years go by. For those who are severely impacted by autism and have no extensive communication skills, there are ways for the people who know the person well to give their observations about the student's likes and dislikes and how those preferences can help shape his future.

Lisa Lieberman, mother of Jordan Ackerson and author of *A Stranger Among Us: Hiring In-Home Support for a Child with Autism Spectrum Disorders and Other Neurological Differences*, believes in teaching children on the spectrum to advocate effectively on their own behalf, in order to develop a sense of potency and influence in their world. Some of the suggestions from Lisa's book include: verbalizing observations about how your child is responding; providing your child with opportunities to make choices; letting your child experience the power of saying no; helping your child recognize his own internal sensations and emotions; and giving your child words to describe how he is feeling.

Lisa told me, "As Jordan grew older, we did much to build a sense of efficacy in his world. We helped him to write a vision statement for his life at age twelve. We encouraged him to write emails to teachers when he felt he wasn't being properly respected by them. We tried to not do too much for him that he was able to accomplish on his own." Lisa makes a crucial point: our children need to learn to stick up for themselves.

Conclusion

Self-advocacy is a needed life skill that should be taught in small steps with the use of a mentor when a child is young. There are various levels of advocacy depending upon age, functioning ability, and need of the person. All students must give input to the IEP process starting at age sixteen. As adults over eighteen, college students must be able to communicate with the college about any accommodations they may need. Disclosure is linked to self-advocacy because self-advocacy becomes necessary when a person's needs are not being met in a given situation. Many adults who were diagnosed as adults believe that children should be told about their own diagnosis. On the topic of disclosure to others, some believe in full disclosure to all, while others choose to disclose only the area of difficulty, or to disclose step by step depending upon the nature of the relationship and the circumstance. Self-awareness is linked to self-advocacy because an individual must be aware of what he is feeling to know what to request in order to get his needs met.

10

Earning a Living

TEACHER: *What would you like to be doing two, five, or ten years from now?*
JEREMY: *Two years roses. Five years working business self-employed.*
    Ten years I do not know.

TEACHER: *What careers are you interested in?*
JEREMY: *No idea. Job would be nice. My job is good. Write about baseball.*

TEACHER: *What would be your ideal job?*
JEREMY: *I want a job outside. Place is important.*

TEACHER: *With your business, what should we do about saving money?*
JEREMY: *I want to save my money for college.*

Jeremy does not like jobs with physical activities but likes to work with ideas and be able to tell others what to do. He wants to do something that would make him famous and thinks writing books would be something he would enjoy doing. As the case manager, I see Jeremy's strong assets like working data, communicating with people to purchase/buy/manage a business. He is able to do gross motor activities, but often finds fine motor activities difficult and

frustrating. Jeremy needs more opportunities exploring jobs and
finding out what he could to have fun and earn money.

These last two ideas are very important to Jeremy.

—Allan Gustafson, interview with Jeremy Sicile-Kira,
spring 2007

In Jeremy's first year of high school, the educator in charge of providing
employment experiences to disabled students did not feel Jeremy was
equipped to work at the community job options she had available. I had
heard about self-employment options for those with developmental disabilities, so Jeremy's teacher, instructional aide, and I got creative. We
helped Jeremy set up his first entrepreneurial experience, delivering sandwiches to teachers on his high school campus. At that time, Jeremy had
very basic communication skills, and he did not appear to have any special
talents or interests, or at least, any that were marketable. We could tell
from his behaviors that he enjoyed moving around, walking around the
local shopping center, and having one-on-one contact with adults. His
teacher, Allan, knew there was a market for providing sandwiches from a
local health food store to teachers bored with on-campus options. For a
year, Jeremy delivered sandwiches, earning a dollar for each sandwich
delivered. He enjoyed putting the order forms in the teachers' mailboxes,
picking up the sandwiches, and developing the rapport he had with the
teachers, who were happy to see him when he delivered their lunches.

His second small business was selling flowers to his high school
peers. By this time, Jeremy could communicate, and he expressed interest in having a business that would put him in contact with his peers and
where he could earn more money. No student organization was selling
flowers on campus, and so Jeremy's instructional aide came up with the
idea, seeing a market and knowing that Jeremy liked flowers. He would
buy roses wholesale then package and sell them individually. It was hard
work; the physical aspects of the job were difficult for Jeremy.

Jeremy needed support for both of these money-making endeavors,
but he already had a one-on-one aide assigned to him because of his
educational, communication, and behavioral needs. Acquiring work

skills was part of his Individualized Educational Program (IEP). Jeremy was very motivated to make money because he wanted an assistant dog as a pet, and I had told him that I was willing to match whatever money he saved toward purchasing the trained dog. He learned valuable economic, business, and marketing lessons from these experiences as well. Best of all, Jeremy's customers saw him and respected him as someone who was providing a needed service in the community, not as a disabled person.

Why Parents and Teachers Need to Be Thinking About Employment Early On

Some readers may wonder what a chapter on earning a living is doing in a book about essential abilities for children to learn. Some parents are still trying to deal with the idea of having a child with autism. Others are hoping to recover their child and think they will never need this chapter. Perhaps, but the subject of skills a person needs to function as an adult— on or off the spectrum—should still be addressed early on. What we learn in childhood, in the school environment, and during the teen years are the foundations for success in the real world of adulthood. For example, my nonautistic teenager, Rebecca, learned organizational and time management skills when she started having school projects in fourth grade that were due the following week, not the next day. She also learned about teamwork and responsibility in school when collaborating on small-group projects. These types of skills are just as important for children on the spectrum, but many are not given the opportunity to learn them, or they don't learn them through the usual channels.

Obviously, there are different ability levels and they do change over time. Someone who is very impacted by autism as a child may be less so when older, due to biomedical and dietary interventions, educational and behavioral therapies, or other strategies. The goal for each child is to reach his or her full potential, whatever that may be, by adulthood. And earning a living is a skill needed by almost everyone.

What we do to earn money is an area that defines us in society. Yet for too many on the autism spectrum, employment is as unattainable as a

walk on the moon. According to the 2002 report by the President's Commission on Excellence in Special Education, 70 percent of disabled
working-age adults are unemployed. According to other reports, those
with autism—including Asperger's syndrome—have an even higher
unemployment rate than other disabled people. Many who do work are
underemployed, meaning they are working at a job that does not make
full use of their abilities or skills. Many, if given proper opportunities and
training, have skills and abilities that would be valuable in appropriate
work settings.

When it comes to changing these disheartening statistics, there are
at least four things that need to be done: prepare our children at an earlier
age for possible employment; do a better job of "marketing" individuals
on the spectrum to prospective employers; teach job coaches about the
autism spectrum and how that relates to work; and start thinking creatively outside the box. Speaking frankly, what we have been doing for
years has apparently not been working, so why do we continue in the
same behavior pattern? As the nonautistic adults, aren't we supposed to
be more flexible and less obsessed with following the rules, that is, doing
something because that's the way we've always done it?

Now that we know so much about helping children on the spectrum,
we need to focus on generalizing or applying our hard-earned knowledge
to the employment/earning-a-living aspect of life. This means, among
other things, helping the child prepare to generalize the essential abilities he has learned by applying them to a work situation: self-awareness
and self-regulation, social relationships, independence (which includes
organizational skills, multitasking, and flexibility), communication, self-
advocacy, and so on—as well as a good dose of self-esteem.

What People on the Spectrum Have to Say

Temple Grandin, who coauthored *Developing Talents: Careers for Individuals with Asperger Syndrome and High Functioning Autism*, presents a lot of
good advice. Temple says that the most important thing jobs require is
that the job holder be willing to work and have a good attitude at work.
She believes strongly that parents should help their child develop his

natural talents, and that young people need mentors to give them guidance and valuable experience.

Many adults on the spectrum choose work based on their interests or special talents. Temple is an animal scientist who designs livestock-handling facilities worldwide, and is an assistant professor of animal sciences at Colorado State University. She is also a frequent lecturer on autism, and has written books and articles on autism as well as animal behavior.

Many other academically gifted adults on the more able end of the spectrum pursue advanced degrees and, after that, opt to stay in the college environment and teach. They enjoy the college atmosphere, which over the course of their studies, becomes familiar. Besides the comforts of familiarity, where else could they get paid for standing up and lecturing for two hours on their favorite topic of interest without getting interrupted? Although there are other aspects of the job they may find challenging, such as the interdepartmental politics and the need for good organizational skills, they are strongly motivated by their passion for their subject area of interest.

Daniel Tammet (*Born on a Blue Day*) runs a successful Web-based business for language tutorials. Language has always been a source of fascination for him, and he is able to learn to speak new languages fluently from scratch in one week.

Michel Crouch, who had the joy of checking the mailbox at home every day when growing up (as described in a previous chapter), is the college postmaster at the Crown College of the Bible in Tennessee.

John Elder Robison, author of *Look Me in the Eye*, credits his Asperger's for giving him a rare insight into electronics. Using that knowledge, he joined a band and eventually ended up designing special effects guitars for KISS in the late 1970s. Afterward he made the leap into a job as an engineer with a major toy and game company, and then moved up the corporate ladder for ten years, until he hit a wall. His undiagnosed Asperger's kept him from fitting into the corporate world; he eventually quit his job and began fixing Mercedes and Land Rover cars in his driveway. From that grew J E Robison Service, one of the most successful independent repair businesses in New England, which is known nationwide for its restoration and customization work, especially on Land Rover, Rolls-Royce, and Bentley vehicles.

Zosia Zaks, who was diagnosed as a result of vocational challenges, says she has worked at every type of job imaginable, including dishwasher, secretary, editor, farmer, cab driver, merchandiser, and telemarketer. In her book *Life and Love*, she provides many good ideas for managing the challenges of the workplace, including a list of suggestions for getting through daily life on the job. Some of these are: select a "work buddy" to help you socially navigate in the workplace; use visual aides such as color codes or a chart to stay organized throughout the day; take notes on the social language that is used on the job; and work tirelessly on communication skills, both verbal and written.

To Disclose or Not to Disclose

Both Temple Grandin and Zosia Zaks write about the complex issue of whether or not a person on the spectrum should disclose the diagnosis of an autism spectrum disorder on the job. Some people opt to disclose their autism at hiring, thus having the right to certain accommodations. However, others prefer not to, and then ask for what they need without mentioning the "A" word. For example, if someone has visual processing challenges triggered by brightly lit environments, the person may say that fluorescent lights give him a headache and ask if it would be okay to modify his cubicle or office.

Most people agree that it is important to gauge for each employment situation whether or not to disclose. Then it is important to figure out how much to disclose and with whom one should share this information. Disclosure in competitive job environments can sometimes work against a person. People on the spectrum are usually not very good at office politics; they are often too honest about their own shortcomings, not realizing that information about areas of difficulties shared with a friendly colleague may be used against them. They may not realize that colleagues who are in line for the same promotion can be cutthroat and may zone in on a person's weak spots and take advantage of them in order to

FOOD FOR THOUGHT

CHILDREN SEVERELY IMPACTED BY AUTISM:
THINKING ABOUT THE FUTURE

Many parents and teachers of the severely impaired feel that advice about looking ahead to future employment is not meant for their children or students. Seriously, having worked with young adults in a state hospital for the developmentally disabled, I realized that despite all my best efforts, my son, Jeremy, was very limited by his functional abilities—before he learned to communicate. The most important things he had going for him were that he was not aggressive and had been taken out into the community every day since he was a baby, and so he had become somewhat sensorially tolerant of the environment around him.

The major difference in my son's life has come from finding a way for him to communicate with us. Now we can ask him about his interests and what he enjoys, what he can be motivated to work at in order to earn money. But to be honest, I was not sitting around waiting for him to finally be able to communicate before trying to figure out what he liked and how we could turn that into his making money when he is older.

I knew that Jeremy, despite all his best efforts and ours, was not going to be a candidate for any kind of community work experience. So I decided to look long and hard at what he liked and thought about what he could do. I attended a few self-employment workshops for the developmentally disabled. Jeremy's teacher was game to try something different.

In observing Jeremy and asking the people who were with him when I wasn't, we came up with a list of things he liked and what he didn't like. He liked riding in cars, listening to music, swimming, walking around campus and the small shopping mall near school, going to visit teachers in classrooms on campus, giving things to people, looking at books, eating, and shopping for food. He did not like sitting for too long, putting things together, sequencing, being in noisy environments, and doing the same thing over and over.

The teacher, who was new to this campus, realized that by Fridays the teachers were sick of the limited choice of food at the school, yet did not have enough time to leave campus, eat, and come back. He suggested Jeremy start a sandwich delivery service on Fridays. I was familiar with the local shops and negotiated a deal with Jimbos, a natural foods grocer, to sell the sandwiches to Jeremy at a cheaper rate. This sandwich delivery service included the things Jeremy liked to do—walking around, visiting the teachers, giving things to people, and shopping—and enabled him to earn money while learning job responsibility and getting positive feedback from the teachers, who were always happy to see him arrive with the sandwiches. As a result, he became a more responsible person and realized he could be productive—and this gave him hope for the future.

Now that Jeremy can write, and we can discuss ideas and interests, he is much more able to consider future employment options. All this is a way of saying that children who do not appear to have special interests or talents (or even many skills) can still earn money. If you look closely and think outside the box, and look at the community needs that exist to see if there is a service your child can provide, the possibilities are there. But Rome wasn't built in a day, so starting to think about the future while your child is young is always helpful.

For more information about the self-employment guide I wrote based on my experiences, see "Customized Employment and Self-Employment as Viable Options," later in this chapter. For current updates, visit my website, www .chantalsicile-kira.com.

get the coveted advancement. On the other hand, disclosure can be useful in avoiding misunderstandings or disappointments in the future—for example, a boss who knows about a valued employee's status on the spectrum might be able to help avoid missed deadlines, communication problems, or other preventable difficulties.

The bottom line, as mentioned in Chapter 9, "Self-Advocacy," is that disclosure is a highly personal decision and is usually based on how much accommodation or modification a person needs in a particular situation.

The Importance of Mentors

Temple Grandin and other adults on the spectrum who have been able to earn a living cite having a mentor as a very important factor in their abil-

PRACTICAL TIP

Before looking for a mentor, think about what it is you want for your child or student. Are you looking for someone who will help develop the social side of your child, or are you looking for someone who will discuss employment opportunities, or both? What kind of time commitment are you looking for—a mentor who is available one hour per week, or twice a month, or less, or more? By defining your expectations, you will have a better idea whom to approach and they will know what their commitment will entail. One word of caution, however. Because potential mentors won't be vetted, unless you know the person well, you would be wise to ensure that a parent, teacher, trusted aide, or tutor is present at all times during mentor-child sessions.

ity to develop a marketable skill in order to find work. As mentioned previously, a mentor is an experienced and trusted adult who is knowledgeable about an area of interest that a student or adult wants to know more about. When it comes to thinking about employment options, imagine that you are the parent of a child who has specific math skills or computer skills or is interested in construction vehicles or trains. And imagine that you are a real estate broker or a cab driver or even a music teacher. No parent or teacher can be expected to be acquainted with and knowledgeable about the vast range of jobs out there that could offer a wealth of opportunity, interest-wise and money-wise, for your child.

If your child appears to have skills or real interest in a specific area, pairing him up with a trusted, knowledgeable person who is willing to be a mentor is a good idea. In grade school, this relationship can offer the child a way to forge a bond outside the family, as well as help the child's self-esteem and offer him an opportunity to practice social skills. Mentors can help a student realize the application of their interests, and help teachers and parents realize the possibilities for the student (for example, the engineering field is vast, but someone in the field can give insight as to what types of education and career options are available).

⊞   ⊞   F O O D   F O R   T H O U G H T   ⊞   ⊞

STARTING MY OWN BUSINESS

Elijah Wapner is a comedian. This is from his presentation at the Talents Within Self-Employment Conference at St. Madeleine Sophie's Center, California, in December 2007. For more information on Elijah, go to www.mrinevitable.com.

My first goal for 11th grade is to run my own business. I have started performing my comedy at different venues around the country, including at many autism conferences. Sometimes I do this as a community service and sometimes I get paid for my presentations and performances. I'm now beginning to learn some basics about small business, and this winter my mom and the ARC (a disability organization) in our community will be supporting me in how to write a business plan, keep books, manage a bank account, book flights and make hotel arrangements. They'll also be supporting me in managing my time and prioritizing tasks as I prepare for my presentations and performances.

⊞   ⊞   ⊞   ⊞   ⊞   ⊞   ⊞   ⊞   ⊞   ⊞   ⊞

Mentors can help a student feel valued as now he has a person who is interested in the same topic he is and is happy to hear the child talk about it (whereas family members might get a bit tired of the subject). Mentors can be good role models as well as help with social aspects of future employment situations. Temple Grandin describes how she had one mentor who explained proper work attire, and another mentor who explained the differences in how you talk to a boss versus how you might speak to a colleague or subordinates. In the short term, the fact that a mentor can converse knowledgeably, and on a regular basis, about the child's special interest is alone a wonderful benefit.

During junior high and then in high school and in transition programs, having a mentor can lead to a possible job or more training or help in college. Neurotypicals do this naturally; we call it networking. We need to help those on the spectrum develop skills, interdependency, and relationships while they are young, so that when they are older, networking will not be an alien concept.

You might have to practice your own networking skills and be a bit creative in finding appropriate mentors. You may find them at school (teachers of particular subjects), in your neighborhood, in your place of worship, or at a local service organization such as your local Toastmasters International or Kiwanis Club. Local trade associations may also be a good place to look. If you are really looking to find out about a field you are unfamiliar with and where you have no contacts but you feel your child may have talents in that area (e.g., informational technology), try calling companies specializing in that field. If you read about someone in the local paper, call him up and ask if you can come and talk to him about what he does and maybe tour his workplace. People love to talk about what they do and will feel complimented by your attention. If your teen has appropriate skills (i.e., can self-regulate), ask if he can tour the place of work, too.

Employment Considerations

When looking at possible jobs or self-employment opportunities for your child or student to pursue, there are many questions to ask yourself. Among them are:

- What is the person interested in or passionate about?
- What is he good at?
- What does he like doing?
- What motivates him?
- Is the person a visual concrete thinker or nonvisual thinker (i.e., good at math, music, and facts)?
- Is the person nonverbal? Verbal? Can he communicate by typing?
- Is he good at organizing or multitasking?
- Is he comfortable having contact with many people or just a few familiar individuals?
- Can the person self-regulate, or does he need to work in a place with low sensory stimulation?

- Does the person like moving around or staying in the same place?
- Can the person handle working forty hours a week, or does he need a part-time job?
- Can he handle working year-round, or does he need seasonal or temporary jobs?

Questions you may wish to ask a perspective employer include:

- Would the employee have control of his environment, or could accommodations or modifications be made in terms of lighting and sound?
- Would the employee have access to a work mentor to help with learning the ropes and to answer any questions?
- If there are job responsibilities that the employee excels at and others that are difficult for him, does the possibility of "job carving" exist—that is, dividing the tasks with another employee so that each person does what he or she is good at?

How to Market the Positive Aspects of
Hiring or Giving Business to an Adult on the Spectrum

Too often, when a professional or parent goes through the traditional means of helping a young person find work, she is asking someone to hire a person with a disability as a good deed or in order to qualify for government incentives rather than emphasizing or "marketing" the positive aspects of hiring someone on the spectrum. However, the reality is that in addition to preparing the job candidate by helping him to research the job requirements and then helping him hone the job-appropriate skills, we also need to develop a business mentality, as opposed to a social worker mentality, in order to effectively "sell" possible employers on the positive attributes the person has.

The Top Ten Skills and Attributes
Most Employers Look For

Let's take a look at the needs of employers as identified by the Bureau of Labor (*Job Outlook 2003*) and see how they relate to possible employees on the spectrum:

1. **Honesty and integrity** is the number one attribute that employers are looking for in prospective employees. This is a very positive attribute that people on the spectrum have. Unless there is another co-diagnosis, people on the spectrum are usually honest to a fault. They don't understand the concept of lying, and they are not the ones you are going to find with their hand in the cash till.

2. **A strong work ethic** is another important attribute that employers want to see. This is another area in which people on the spectrum shine—how many children or teens on the spectrum do you know that stick to a schedule religiously every day? These are not workers that are going to call in sick or arrive late because they were out having one too many tequila shots the night before.

3. **Analytical skills** are highly rated by prospective employers. What we parents tend to think of as obsessive attention to detail is really a positive attribute in terms of being able to stay focused and looking at things in detail. The obsession that many of us find so annoying at times is actually a much-needed talent that employers value.

4. **Computer skills** are a necessity for many of today's jobs, and many on the spectrum have a knack for them. Granted, we need to find out how to channel that computer knowledge into a marketable field. That's one area where mentors can help.

5. **Teamwork**, meaning that someone works well with others, is also a valued competence that potential employers look for. At first glance this may seem a difficult area for many of those

on the spectrum, but in reality if rules are established and it is very clear who is responsible for what, and when something is due to which particular person, then someone on the spectrum can be quite good at teamwork. Another way to make this easier (and that can be suggested to a prospective employer) is to designate one person on the team as the "go to" person with whom the person on the spectrum exchanges information, ensuring no miscommunication or missing of important tasks or deadlines.

6. **Time management and organizational skills** do not come naturally to everyone on the spectrum, although some are very organized. This is a skill area that is much needed in all areas of a person's life including schoolwork for those who are integrated, and everyday living skills for everyone, including those who need one-on-one aides. These skills need to be taught from an early age, to kids on the spectrum as well as neurotypical kids.

7. **Communication skills (oral and written)** are indeed valued by employers. Often we think of communication skills as being extremely difficult for those on the spectrum, and it is true for many. However, there are examples of those on the spectrum who have excelled in fields where communication is extremely important (Michael John Carley was a playwright and diplomat before becoming executive director of GRASP, Kamran Nazeer is a British government policy maker, Sean Barron is a journalist, and Elijah Wapner is a comedian). More and more, we are seeing young adults who are considered severely impacted by autism learn to communicate by typing. So again, this skill is not one that all on the spectrum possess, but many do—and everyone should be encouraged to find and develop his voice, no matter what medium he uses to express it.

8. **Flexibility** is often difficult for individuals on the spectrum. However, this skill is required not only for many jobs but also in all areas of life, and it should be taught early on, as explained

PRACTICAL TIP

Review this "Top Ten" list with your child or student in mind. Analyze the skills you think he may have, and those that are more difficult for him. Many of these skills are also needed in school. Think of what you've read in earlier chapters and how you can teach or practice the skill areas that need improvement.

in previous chapters. As soon as a child has learned rules or sequences and knows them well, he should be taught what to do when circumstances change (i.e., when a rule is broken or doesn't apply, or something is missing in a sequence).

9. **Interpersonal skills**, or working well with others, is another area that is valued by employers, and which can be difficult for many on the spectrum. This is not just a work requirement; it is a skill set necessary for daily living, so that we can function in our homes, schools, and communities. It is never too early to begin to teach these all-important skills.

10. **Motivation/initiative** is an area that people on the spectrum can excel in *if* the work they do is in one of their areas of interest or involves something they like to do, whether it be working with maps or numbers, or just repeatedly folding pizza boxes. Again, as for all of us, finding work in an area of interest is a big motivator for getting the job done. (Yes, I can hear some of you thinking, "But *I* hate my job and I still have to do it!" However, most neurotypicals have other things going on in their lives that give them pleasure: families, relationships friends, hobbies.) For someone on the spectrum, her job may be the only activity and connection to the world that she has. For this reason, it is important to ensure she is working at something she enjoys. For employers, having an employee who is passionate about what he or she does is a real asset.

Customized Employment and
Self-Employment as Viable Options

Customized employment has become a viable option for many with developmental disabilities, including those on the autism spectrum. There are many states that have initiatives in place to encourage a more creative look at work possibilities as they realize that the models currently out there, including supported employment, do not seem to be working for the majority of developmentally disabled individuals who could be earning money.

Customized employment means that the work is tailored to the individual, not the other way around. It can mean job carving, where one job is carved up into different tasks and shared by several people. This allows for those who excel in certain areas and are challenged by others to do the part of a job that fits their skill set. Another type of customized employment is self-employment (sometimes referred to as micro-enterprise), which basically means having your own small business or working for yourself. The business can be one that provides a service (consulting is an example) or a product. This can be an attractive option to those who are having a difficult time fitting into a regular paid position.

Self-Employment

Throughout this book you have been hearing from some adults who are authors and speakers. There are also developmentally disabled adults around the country (including some more impacted by autism) who run businesses. Some examples include: Johnson Recycling, created by Justin Johnson, who wanted to help the environment (his motto: Crush Aluminum Cans Not the Environment); Dusty's Puppets, an entertainer who loves putting on puppet shows for children; Lizz's Food for Thought, a coffee and food delivery service for staff meetings and trainings started by Elizabeth Garvey (Lizz). Other examples can be found at www.farnorthernrc.org/selfadvocacyrocks/Adventures_In_Business/Adventures.htm.

When looking at self-employment as an option, some of the things to be thinking about include:

- Does the person have difficulty with sensory processing (i.e., cannot handle too much light, noise, or people), and is self-regulating difficult for him?
- Does he have an interest or talent that leads to a marketable service or product, or could he fill a consumer need?
- Does the person have access to a business support team if she is not independent?
- Does the person need to start earning money right away?
- Does he have a "day job" he can keep while starting up his business?

While Jeremy was in high school, he started learning about self-employment through the hands-on experience of selling a needed service (delivering sandwiches to teachers who had no time to leave campus) and a needed product (selling flowers to peers at school where no flowers were available on campus). By actually doing the business, Jeremy learned valuable lessons including: the cost of doing business; the difference between a profit and a loss; and how marketing, location, and price affected the numbers of customers he was able to attract and keep. Jeremy also learned that if there was a part of the job he could not do, he had to pay someone else to do it—another cost of doing business.

Another useful aspect of looking into the self-employment option is that going through the process of analyzing which activities and interest areas the person likes and dislikes can sometimes lead to discovering areas of traditional employment they had not thought of previously. It can also lead to valuable contacts in the business community, who might even have a position to offer, either now or in the future.

Basic Guidelines for Self-Employment

One challenge that those who are not business owners face is a lack of knowledge about how you go about setting up and running your own

PRACTICAL TIP

Self-employment is not for everyone—on or off the spectrum. It is important to determine whether the individual is a good candidate for self-employment. Consider:

- Is the person self-motivated by a passion and/or by a desire to make money?
- Does he have the staying power to stick through the first year or two when things may be slow and dicey?
- Does the person have a few reliable family members, friends, or mentors—who will serve as his Business Support Team to guide him through a business plan, marketing analysis, and so forth?
- Is this Business Support Team able to help him identify resources and other professionals who can help, if needed?
- Is the person willing to do/learn the skills needed, or able to barter/pay for the skills someone else will have to do?
- Does the person, or someone on the team, understand the importance and need for marketing in order to attract new business?

If the person does not have family or supportive people who are reliable, it will be difficult to be successfully self-employed unless the person is highly motivated, independent, and functionally able.

business. Most of us think of having or running a business as a scary prospect with no stability. However, the reality is that not many jobs have much stability anymore, and as the unemployment rate is so high for people on the spectrum, self-employment is worth looking into.

Many states, including California, have started self-employment initiatives. The San Diego Regional Center recently offered self-employment grants funded by the Department of Developmental Services, enabling organizations to offer self-employment options as part of the services available to adults and teenagers transitioning to adulthood. I developed *A Beginner's Guide to Self-Employment*, a workbook that is in use at the Self-Employment Program at St. Madeleine Sophie's Center (a day program for adults), and is also included in the curriculum for the Transition Resources for Adult Community Education (TRACE) Program of the San Diego Unified School District. Here are some suggestions for getting started on self-employment.

Interest Inventory

When looking for ideas of possible ways to make money, think about the potential entrepreneur's likes and dislikes as well as possible talents. The person needs to consider:

1. What do you like to do in your free time?
2. What makes you happy?
3. What don't you like to do?
4. Do you like: Quiet? Calm? Music? Noise? Crowds? Few people around?
5. What are you good at doing?
6. How many days/hours do you want to work?
7. Whom do you see being in your circle of support?
8. Where do you want to work from?
9. Do you like to make things with your hands?
10. Do you like working on the computer?
11. Do you like moving around or staying in the same place?
12. What are your strengths?
13. What are your interests?
14. Do you get overwhelmed easily?
15. How do you react when you are overwhelmed?

Market Needs/Community Needs

Following the interest inventory, brainstorming with people in the geographical area or with some expertise in an identified field (if there is one) can generate ideas as to market needs that could relate to some of the criteria established in the Interest Inventory. For those who want to establish a local business, the needs of the immediate community must be analyzed.

Role of the Business Support Team

The Circle of Support includes one-on-one support, family caregivers, friends, former teachers, neighbors, community members, businesspeople, and mentors: anyone who knows the individual well. Different people can fulfill different roles, but these roles need to be filled:

1. Give input on Interest Inventory.
2. Give input on strengths and weaknesses.
3. Teach business and other skills.
4. Mentor the person.
5. Encourage development of business communication skills and self-regulation.
6. Locate professionals who can help if needed.
7. Locate resources if needed.
8. Ensure that the proper paperwork is done.

Idea/Concept Development

Once an area of interest has been discovered and some brainstorming has occurred, one or more ideas and concepts will come to mind for a business. This needs to sit/gel for a while, maybe others explored, and then when a person is really enthused by an idea or concept, continue on to theoretically developing the idea into a business.

Basic Understanding of Doing Business

These concepts need to be taught while developing the business:

1. Business expenses (e.g., paper bags/napkins for sandwich delivery service)
2. Profit and loss (e.g., flowers ruined through stimming cannot be sold = loss)
3. Marketing (people need to know you exist to buy from you)
4. Location important (can they find you?)

FOOD FOR THOUGHT

MY BUSINESSES

This is from a presentation by Jeremy Sicile-Kira at the Talents Within Self-Employment Conference at St. Madeleine Sophie's Center, California, in December 2007. For more information on Jeremy, go to www.jeremysicile-kira.com.

My name is Jeremy Sicile-Kira. I am eighteen years old. I am in a transition program. I want to go to college, but I need to make money first. I want to write a book about my life experiences. I have had two small businesses to earn money. I saved the money to get my assistant dog, Handsome. I want people to know you can develop the business you want, when you have the courage, and the time, to dedicate to the things you like in life.

My first business was delivering sandwiches to staff on Fridays at my high school. I got the sandwiches from Jimbos for a dollar less than I sold to the teachers. So I made a dollar on each sandwich.

I started a business selling flowers to students at my high school at lunch time on Fridays. The hardest part of the business was getting help with putting the flowers together. It was difficult because being disabled I needed a lot of help. The easiest part was picking out the flowers. The best part about the business was getting stopped by other students at recess to see if I was selling flowers for lunch.

Here is what I wrote for my Economics class about how economics relates to my flower business:

The less you sell the less you make.
You must take in more than you spend.
The number of buyers is related to the amount they are willing to spend.
Money plays an important part in everyone's life.

I enjoyed the sandwich business more than the flower business because it was easier. But, if I could start up either business tomorrow, I would pick flowers because I earned more money.

Informal Market Survey

1. Does this product/service exist already in the community?
2. How will this one be better/different?
3. How much does the other one go for?
4. How much did it cost to get started?
5. What about location, location, location?
6. Ask people you know/don't know if they would use it, why, and how much they are willing to pay.

Market Analysis (Formalizing/Concretizing the Idea)

1. Where/what is the industry (food, service, etc.)?
2. Who are your customers and how much will they pay?
3. Who are your competitors and what is your edge?

Business Plan Development (Simplified to Start)

1. Concept or idea
   a. Name and location of business
   b. Purpose of business (i.e., mission statement)
   c. Who are the customers?
2. Assets/equity—things the person will bring to the business that will benefit the business (e.g., transportation vehicle, computer, needed supplies)
3. Support people who are needed to make the business happen— and whether or not they are paid—for example:
   a. One-on-one aide—paid
   b. Mentor from community—unpaid
4. Cost of business—the details
   a. Equipment
   b. Paid supports
   c. Marketing/advertising
   d. Professional advice

5. List any "job carving," that is, parts to be done by someone else or another business
   a. Product
   b. Service
   c. Task
6. Possible resources for funding
7. Calendar: an analysis of tasks to be done in a month

Marketing

I can't emphasize enough how important the marketing aspect of any business is. No matter how great a product or service is, the business will not survive unless people—potential customers—know about it.

Doing the Necessary Legal Paperwork—Action Plan

Someone on the Business Support Team will need to take responsibility to make sure the legal paperwork necessary to set up a business is properly filled out and filed. Check with your local city hall about what needs to be done in your area. Another great resource with offices all around the United States and free help online is SCORE (Service Corps of Retired Executives), a service of the US Small Business Administration. This is a good source of free information and might also be helpful in finding a mentor.

Conclusion

How your child will earn a living as an adult is not necessarily the main thing you are thinking about when he is still young. However, it is important to have an understanding about how all the life skills he is learning relate to adult life. Most people on the spectrum are either unemployed or underemployed, which means we need to rethink our approach to the job market. Looking at the Top Ten Skills employers are looking for when hiring can give us an idea of what skills our children need in order to have a chance in the job market of tomorrow, and they even lend themselves to some potential "selling points" for those on the spectrum. Customized employment is an option for many, including self-employment.

Closing Comments

TEACHER: *When somebody works with you, what do you look for?*
JEREMY: *To know my likes, to be kind, not to be too busy to take time to know me. I like people to be calm, walk slow, and teach fast.*

—Allan Gustafson, interview with Jeremy Sicile-Kira,
for 2006 ITP Meeting

Recently one morning I opened the door to Jeremy's room so that Handsome, Jeremy's assistant dog, could jump on the bed and wake Jeremy as usual. When I saw my son about ten minutes later, he was grinning from ear to ear. "Jeremy," I asked, "why do you have such a big smile on your face this morning?" Using his litewriter, he replied, "Because I had a nice dream." "So, what was it about?" I asked. "I dreamed I could talk, but then I remembered I couldn't," Jeremy answered. "That sounds sad, so why are you smiling?" I asked. Jeremy replied, "Because then I remembered I could type."

As I finish writing this book, there are four people in the news whom my mind keeps wandering off to think about. The first is Jean Dominique Bauby, the editor-in-chief of *Elle* who suffered a stroke in his forties and lapsed into a coma in December 1995. When he woke up twenty days later, he was mentally aware of his surroundings but physi-cally paralyzed with the exception of some movement in his head and left eye. Bauby had locked-in syndrome, a rare condition caused by stroke damage to the brain stem. Bauby wrote his memoir, *The Diving Bell and the Butterfly*, by using only his left eye, blinking out a code representing the letters of the alphabet.

The movie (which won the Director's Award at the Cannes Film Fes-tival in the spring of 2007), which is based on the book, has just been released here in the States, which is why he is back in the news a bit. Bauby died soon after the book was published in 1997.

I am thinking about this now, because I cannot imagine a fate worse than not being able to communicate. It signifies true imprisonment. Yet, here was a man who could only move his left eye, and he wrote a book. It was a speech therapist who found a way for him to communicate his thoughts. I can't help thinking that if Bauby had not been a creative, intel-ligent, well-liked man, admired by many and in a position of power, would anyone have tried so hard to figure out a way for him to communicate?

And I think of all the people with autism I know who have their own kind of "locked-in syndrome"—those whom we have not yet provided with a way to communicate. We don't know what they are thinking or what they are capable of. Because of people like Sue Rubin and Tito and DJ Savarese and Jeremy, and all the others I've heard about who have found an alternative means of communication rather than speech, I have hope that we will one day be able to help the rest. Like Bauby's therapist, we must assume intelligence, and then we will try harder to find a way for them to become unlocked, so that their voices will shine through and be heard, regardless of their level of functioning.

Then, I find myself thinking of Heather Kuzmich, twenty-one, who was one of thirteen young women selected by supermodel Tyra Banks to compete on the popular reality television show *America's Next Top Model* in the fall of 2007. Heather has Asperger's syndrome. A gifted art stu-dent from Valparaiso, Indiana, she was voted the viewer favorite eight weeks in a row, making her one of the most popular contestants in the show's four-and-a-half-year history. Heather got high marks for her photos from the professionals involved and made it to the top five. What got her knocked off the show are typical Aspie challenges: communication (she flubbed her lines while filming a commercial), organization, and orientation mobility—she got hopelessly lost in Beijing, meeting up with only one out of five fashion designers she was supposed to visit with.

I'm not usually a big fan of reality shows, but Heather is a great role model. It took a lot of nerve to go through all that the show entailed— the application process, living in the house with other girls (some of them a bit catty) whom she was competing against, and having a film crew around all the time. The best part is, with the help of a Business Support Team, she will no doubt have a terrific modeling career ahead of her and will become even more of an inspiring success story to others on the spectrum.

Jamie Smith, an autistic young man from Chicago, went to China to compete as a power lifter at the Special Olympics World Games. He had been nominated by his longtime coach, Rob DeSanto. Jamie had already won dozens of medals and he worked two jobs. Besides competing, he had to make the long trip there. Unfortunately, his longtime coach passed away unexpectedly, shortly before the competition. Yet Jamie made it to Shanghai and performed well. Displaying perfect form, he medaled in each lift—bronze in the squat, bronze in the dead lift, silver in the bench press—and he won silver for the overall competition.

Jason "J-Mac" McElwain is the autistic basketball player who scored twenty points in the final minutes of the last high school basketball game of the season in February 2006. Jason is back in the news as the book he cowrote with Daniel Paisner has just been published. Jason became an inspiration to millions of people, on and off the spectrum, was invited to appear on *Oprah*, won an ESPY award, and even met the president. In reading his book, *The Game of My Life*, it is apparent that Jason has been surrounded most of his life by an outstanding support group: parents who did a great job raising him; his brother Josh, who included him in all his activities; and a community of caring people—neighbors, classmates, teammates, and coaches—who not only accepted him but also encouraged him to be the best he could be.

We need to hear and see more stories of people on the spectrum who, like Heather, Jamie, and Jason, put themselves out there and reach for the stars. We need to hear more about the family, friends, and communities who have given people like them the supportive and encouraging environment that allows them to work toward making their dream a reality.

Fortunately, life is better for people on the spectrum than it was twenty or even ten years ago. There is more awareness, and there are more opportunities than ever before. There are therapies, diets, biomedical treatments, and strategies to help with sensory challenges and other difficulties. There is still a lot to be done. But with all that we know now, we can teach children the basic skills they need to live to the best of their abilities, to reach their potential, and to have a productive, fun, and happy life in a world that is more accepting of their differences.

RESOURCES

There are many resources available to help people on the spectrum and their families. Here are some of them, listed in alphabetical order under the appropriate heading.

Autism Organizations

Autism Committee (AUTCOM): www.autcom.org
Autism Hub: www.autism-hub.co.uk
Autism One: www.autismone.org
Autism Research Institute (ARI): www.autism.com
Autism Society of America (ASA): www.autism-society.org
Autism Speaks: www.autismspeaks.org
Global and Regional Asperger Partnership (GRASP): www.grasp.org
Helping Autism through Learning and Outreach (HALO): www.halo-soma.org
MAAP Services: www.maapservices.org
National Autism Association: www.nationalautismassociation.org
National Autistic Society (NAS): www.nas.org.uk
Organization for Autism Research (OAR): www.researchautism.org
Safe Minds: www.safeminds.org
Talk About Curing Autism (TACA): www.talkaboutcuringautism.org
Unlocking Autism: www.unlockingautism.org
World Autism Organization: www.worldautism.org

Autism-Related Media

Age of Autism: www.ageofautism.com

Autism Advocate: www.autism-society.org/site/PageServer?pagename=
  AdvocateMagazine

Autism-Asperger's Digest Magazine: www.autismdigest.com

Autism Calendar: www.sarnet.org/events

Autism File: www.autismfile.com

Autism One Radio: www.autismone.org/radio

Autism Spectrum Quarterly: www.asquarterly.com

Healing Thresholds Autism eBrief: http://autism.healingthresholds.com

Schafer Autism Report: www.sarnet.org

Spectrum Magazine: http://spectrumpublications.com

Valerie's List: www.valerieslist.com

Employment Resources and Information

AUTIES.ORG: www.auties.org

Autism Making a Difference: www.autismmakingadifference.com

Income Links: www.incomelinks.biz

Griffin-Hammis Associates: www.griffinhammis.com

SCORE: www.score.org

Sherry Beamer and Associates: www.sbeamerassoc.com

ENDNOTES

1. Williams, Donna. (1998) *Like Colour to the Blind: Soul Searching and Soul Finding*. London: Jessica Kingsley Publishers.
2. Donna Williams' Blog. "Touching the heaven of shared social; a memory of Bernard Rimland," November 22, 2006. http://blog.donnawilliams.net/2006/11/22/touching-the-heaven-of-shared-social-a-memory-of-bernard-rimland (accessed May 8, 2008).
3. Zaks, Zosia. (2006) *Life and Love: Positive Strategies for Autistic Adults*. Shawnee Mission, KS: Autism Asperger Publishing Company, p. 9.
4. King, Brian R. "Brian's Asperger's." http://web.mac.com/brianrking/Im_An_Aspie/Brians_Aspergers.html (accessed May 8, 2008).
5. Grandin, Temple, and Sean Barron. (2005) *The Unwritten Rules of Social Relationships: Decoding Social Mysteries Through the Unique Perspectives of Autism*. Arlington, TX: Future Horizons, p. 44.
6. Nazeer, Kamran. (2007) *Send in the Idiots: Stories from the Other Side of Autism*. London: Bloomsbury Publishing, p. 22.
7. Rubin, Sue. "The Impact of Communication on Behavior as Experienced by a Non-verbal Person," presentation, July 12, 2007. The Autism Society of America's 38th National Conference on Autism Spectrum Disorders (July 11–14, 2007). http://asa.confex.com/asa/2007/techprogram/S2791.HTM (accessed May 8, 2008).
8. Dubin, Nick. (2007) *Asperger Syndrome and Bullying: Strategies and Solutions*. London: Jessica Kingsley Publishers.
9. Williams, Donna. Donna Williams' Blog: "Autistic achievements—Donna Williams, newly qualified expert bath runner," October 18, 2006.

http://blog.donnawilliams.net/2006/10/18/donna-williams-newly-qualified-expert-bath-runner (accessed May 8, 2008).

10. Grandin, Temple, and Sean Barron. (2005) *The Unwritten Rules of Social Relationships: Decoding Social Mysteries Through the Unique Perspectives of Autism.* Arlington, TX: Future Horizons, pp. 3, 60, 62.

11. Holliday Willey, Liane. (1999) *Pretending to Be Normal: Living with Asperger's Syndrome.* London: Jessica Kingsley Publishers.

12. King, Brian R. "Brian's Asperger's." http://web.mac.com/brianrking/Im_An_Aspie/Brians_Aspergers.html (accessed May 8, 2008).

13. Shore, Stephen, ed. (2004) *Ask and Tell: Self-Advocacy and Disclosure for People on the Autism Spectrum.* Shawnee Mission, KS: Autism Asperger Publishing Company, pp. 67–68.

14. Shore, Stephen, ed. (2004) *Ask and Tell: Self-Advocacy and Disclosure for People on the Autism Spectrum.* Shawnee Mission, KS: Autism Asperger Publishing Company, pp. 33, 62.

INDEX

Index

ABOUT THE AUTHOR

Chantal Sicile-Kira is an international speaker and advocate who has been involved with autism spectrum disorders for more than twenty years as both a parent and a professional. She is the founder of Autism: Making a Difference, which provides consultation services. Chantal served on the Taskforce on Transitional Services and Supports reporting to the California Legislative Blue Ribbon Commission on Autism. Her first book, *Autism Spectrum Disorders*, was the recipient of the 2005 Autism Society of America's Outstanding Literary Work of the Year Award as well as a San Diego Book of the Year Award for Best in Health. Her second book, *Adolescents on the Autism Spectrum*, received the 2006 San Diego Book of the Year Award for Best in Health/Fitness. A former researcher on BBC documentaries and a line producer on a television series in Paris, Chantal currently hosts a weekly radio show, "The Real World of Autism," on Autism One Radio and writes for various publications, including an "Ask Chantal" column for *The Autism File*, and blogs occasionally on the *Huffington Post*. Chantal's family has been highlighted in *Newsweek* and featured on the MTV documentary *True Life* series in the award-winning segment "I Have Autism." For more information, visit www.chantalsicile-kira.com.

T103.1109

PO #: 4500354191